Praise for *Teacher in the C*

Lisa Jane Ashes' beautifully crafted exploration of the difficul⁣ ⁣ ⁣ ⁣ ⁣ ⁣ ⁣ ⁣ ⁣ ⁣ and students is thoroughly enjoyable. As well as exploring these challenges from a variety of insightful perspectives, Lisa shares a wealth of accessible strategies and signposts which will directly support teaching professionals in their daily work.

A refreshing blend of reality, hope, humour, compassion and pragmatic solutions, *Teacher in the Cupboard* resets the moral compass and hands educators a road map to purposeful teaching and learning.

Barry Dunn, Head of Religious Studies, Seaham High School

Lisa Jane Ashes' *Teacher in the Cupboard* is a truthful and heartfelt reflection on the realities of the teaching profession – every teacher will recognise a little bit of themselves in the scenarios described.

From time to time we all find ourselves in challenging and tricky situations – and therefore the need for self-awareness and evaluation is critical for teachers. Lisa has clearly taken note of this necessity and in this book offers many practical strategies to help facilitate reflective thinking. She prompts us to really observe and listen to what is happening around us, and poses probing questions we should ask ourselves when children appear to disengage from their learning.

Teacher in the Cupboard will offer similar comfort to that of the friendly colleague in the staffroom, who we can all turn to when we need a little guidance.

Katy Hodges, Assistant Head Teacher and SENCO, Westfield School

At last, a voice that puts people back into education. I for one am tired of the 'system' and its inherent fear with its managers, inspectors, know-it-alls and education ministers being the domineering naysayers of our schools. Lisa is on the money when she says that what we do requires us all to see the humanity in one another. Education will be richer as a result. The book's subtitle, 'Self-reflective, solution-focused teaching and learning', is a worthy reminder that the teaching profession is a human endeavour, often forgotten in the milieu of modern education.

Teacher in the Cupboard challenges us to reflect on what the problems in our contexts are – and on the excuses we make for not resolving them – and encourages us to think creatively to find workable and humane solutions. It is filled with calm and level-headed examples of problem-solving, from tackling difficult classes and reluctant learners to managing our frantic workloads. Lisa is unshakeably positive in her outlook, even when reflecting on teaching's difficult moments – insisting that a solution can always be found within ourselves if we just stop, look and listen. She also offers ideas around why and how difficulties arise, and how we can find pre-emptive solutions that enable us to be more productive and our students better behaved and better learners.

At the heart of Lisa's approach are the relationships teachers build between themselves and their students. The neat, succinct examples of what this might look, sound and feel like offer excellent opportunities to reflect on your own practice as well as that of those you work alongside.

Teacher in the Cupboard is instantly useable for expert and beginner teachers alike. Lisa's honesty and positivity make it an enjoyable, humbling and useful read, and one that I will return to again and again in reflecting upon and refining my practice.

Darren Mead, teacher and author of *The Expert Teacher*

I think Lisa Jane Ashes' 'self-blindness' metaphor is appropriate for any teacher. We are never too old to learn new things about ourselves or how to handle situations, and *Teacher in the Cupboard* advocates just that. It's practical, easy to follow, and grounded in real-life examples, which makes its ideas and suggestions both reliable and easy to action. It also offers some fresh ideas about how to deal with staff, and how to approach them when an issue arises.

I felt like Lisa was coaching me personally throughout this book, and it's made me reflect on a few situations I have found myself in – whether with staff or with students – that I would want to handle differently. I now feel invigorated and ready to tackle my trickier classes, taking greater care to reflect on how I can adapt my practice to better manage behaviour and ensure I'm fully stretching my learners.

Teacher in the Cupboard would be a particularly encouraging read for newly qualified teachers, to help them develop the high levels of reflection needed to enhance students' behaviour for learning.

Kathy Howell, English Faculty Leader, Caludon Castle Teaching School

TEACHER
IN THE CUPBOARD

Self-reflective, solution-focused teaching and learning

LISA JANE ASHES

independent
thinking press

First published by

Independent Thinking Press
Crown Buildings, Bancyfelin, Carmarthen, Wales, SA33 5ND, UK
www.independentthinkingpress.com
and
Independent Thinking Press
PO Box 2223, Williston, VT 05495, USA
www.crownhousepublishing.com

Independent Thinking Press is an imprint of Crown House Publishing Ltd.

First published 2019.

British Library Cataloguing-in-Publication Data
A catalogue entry for this book is available from the British Library.

Print ISBN 978-178135296-0
Mobi ISBN 978-178135324-0
ePub ISBN 978-178135325-7
ePDF ISBN 978-178135326-4

LCCN 2018968073

Printed and bound in the UK by
TJ International, Padstow, Cornwall

For Tony, Miesha and Samuel.

FOREWORD

I have to admit, I never thought I'd see Lisa Jane Ashes telling people to get back in the closet. I still remember the evening when the improbable title of this book was born. Lisa was sitting across from me and Independent Thinking's Ian Gilbert in a bar in Manchester when she announced that she'd been relegated to a cupboard during her first term of assisting an English teacher. 'It was quite a large cupboard,' she reassured me, as she sipped on her pint and beheld my horrified expression. 'I guess the teacher just *really* didn't want an assistant.'

Of course, I immediately wanted to express righteous indignation on my friend's behalf – in a 'Nobody-puts-Baby-in-a-corner' sort of way. After all, Lisa's skills as a teacher, mentor and trainer have long since been proven. But Lisa's perception of the situation was casually philosophical: 'It was ok …' she shrugged, 'I just used the time to watch and think and learn as much as possible about what could be done.'

A quote alleged to be by psychiatrist Viktor E. Frankl, or maybe even Stephen Covey, provides precious insight to life: 'Between stimulus and response there is space. In that space is our power to choose our response. In our response lies our growth and our freedom.' For Lisa, this 'space', this priceless moment of stepping back, breathing and observing before reacting, is where the power lies, not just for us as teachers, but as parents, managers, colleagues and friends. This *space* offers us the chance to explore and acknowledge the undercurrents of a problem and to shine a light on our own attitudes. This exquisite, underused space is what Lisa affectionately calls 'the cupboard'.

And that's how Lisa approaches problems – in this book and in life: not with trepidation, or rash reaction, or even dogged determination, but instead with a period of considered and gentle curiosity before taking any action at all. Unlike those staffroom dementors we've all encountered at some point in our careers, Lisa doesn't see problems as a nuisance, a buzzkill, a frigging pain in the backside. When she encounters a tricky situation, she pauses and simply says, 'Hmmm … This is *interesting* …'

Fast forward from the Mancunian bar by several years and Lisa and I are working on charity projects in Nepal and Uganda, where difficulties present themselves almost hourly – from man-eating mosquitoes to child-caning teachers. As a privileged co-worker, I've witnessed Lisa braving her way through a myriad of complex setbacks, defusing rows between volunteers and uniting the most unlikely companions in a common goal. Her willingness to bypass fear and find the key to manipulate an apparently insurmountable problem into a tremendous opportunity for learning and growth has often been a great source of amusement (as well as relief!) to me. It's not that Lisa doesn't *feel* fear, it's that she sort of *takes it with her* … So I think it's fair to say that over the years I have come to see Lisa as the trickster imp of the teaching community; a Geordie Puck in the great Forest of Education. And not just because she's five foot two … but also because she whispers into the ears of educators with her quick-witted inspiration: 'You can see this another way. You can feel and experience this differently.' Indeed, in this book, she sabotages the factory setting of 'I am powerless, I am helpless, I am the hapless recipient of this situation,' and sets into motion the cogs of innovation, empowerment and breakthrough, making delightful mischief of our tendency to stay in our comfort zones.

This is all well and good, but can you really trust a narrator who ended up leaving a perfectly good teaching and consulting job to pursue action research into the most difficult aspects of teaching … by becoming a *supply teacher*! Who in their right mind would *elect* to lose their power? Who would *choose* a position perceived as inferior in the eyes of many staff and students? I mean, isn't that a little bit masochistic or just, well, crazy?

But Lisa knows she didn't sign up for power and superiority. In fact, I think she went into teaching in the same open-minded way she went into that northern tattoo shop: 'I don't know what's going to happen here, but let's just experiment and see what takes form. Go ahead and decorate me.'

And she's right about supply teaching being a perfect place to explore the nuances of real problem-solving in schools. After all, every NQT knows how frustrating it feels when a long-established teacher tells you, 'I never have any trouble with behaviour' – and you just can't quite work out what it is they *do* that transforms that class-from-hell into a choir of little cherubs. Often, of course, it's simply because the teacher's reputation precedes them and therefore it's not a formula you can bottle and roll out to other teachers. When your reputation precedes you, you can achieve all sorts of astounding results. It's why Ariana Grande can stick a pair of cat ears on her head and start a worldwide fashion craze; whereas if I'd tried to be the originator of feline headbands, people would quite probably have just felt sorry for me. Lisa stuck herself in the line of fire and built her solution-focused approach to teaching from ground zero. No rock-star status, no friends in high places, not even a modest teaching and learning responsibility (TLR).

So why is a solution-based approach so sorely needed in schools right now? Well, consider the gradual stripping away of teacher autonomy that has taken place over the last few decades. Longstanding teachers often tell me that they remember when they could 'choose' what to teach and so would select something which fired them with enthusiasm and passion that they could transmit to their learners. Now they lament that they often feel they must simply wait for instruction about what to teach and how to teach it – down to the last prescribed lesson plan, activity and resource. But do we want to fill our schools with obedient recipients, rather than innovative creators? Technicians who will simply *deliver* the curriculum, rather than conceive of and give *birth* to it? Because if creative teaching isn't valued then it obviously won't be honed and developed, and so, as a terrifying consequence, creative problem-solving and an internal locus of control may fall by the wayside too.

I catch a glimpse of this scary phenomenon sometimes when I'm working with teachers to develop their classroom practice. An earnest teacher will approach me during the break and tell me, 'I'd love to try that strategy you showed us, but unfortunately we're not allowed to move the children around. They have to stay sitting in their "ability groups" and they have to be organised boy, girl, boy, girl. That's school policy.' Sadly, there's an implication in this 'school policy' that the teacher's professional judgement is not to be trusted and they must work instead within parameters dictated by someone who probably does not intricately know the children and their needs. And sometimes teacher disempowerment is even more striking: teachers have said to me, 'I loved the exercise you demonstrated where the students make the question cards, but we don't have card available in my school – only paper. Would it be okay for them to write on paper instead of card?' This uncertainty about whether it's acceptable to deviate *in any way* from a given idea, to independently problem-solve or creatively adapt without seeking permission, is, in my opinion, quite alarming. There should surely be an in-built right for educators of the next generation to be just a little rebellious.

Perhaps problem-solving and perceptive analysis have not been adequately valued or cultivated in teachers because it's far harder to measure those skills than it is to measure teachers' performance by their students' test results. And we do like to measure things, don't we? A teacher's ability to inspire, care, innovate and view problems from multiple perspectives is extremely difficult to quantify. We are right to fear that the 'teach-to-the-test' approach murders the broadness of the curriculum and the creativity of learners; but what if there's another more insidious, more horrifying impact? What if that approach is also whittling away the self-governing skills of us teachers?

Lisa reminds us all that, as experts in our field, we need to know we have the right to a voice and a vision of our own. We need to have autonomy and we need to make sure that our decisions are driven by curiosity rather than fear, by exploration rather than comfort and by solution-seeking rather than self-reproach or ego. Is this kind of 'time out' in 'the cupboard' a comfortable notion? No. Is it the easiest option? No. But, is it a sure-fire way to rapidly grow as a practitioner? Yes. Yes. Yes.

Isabella Wallace

ACKNOWLEDGEMENTS

Thank you to every colleague and teacher far and wide who has contributed, perhaps unknowingly, to my learning journey. Whether you were the teacher who put me in a cupboard, a learning mentor who modelled compassion, my mentor, my line manager, a nameless teacher in the staffroom or a mate who drank cups of tea with me on a Friday, without you, this book would not have been possible.

Thank you to the wonderful Jane Hewitt for being so patient with me as I messed about in so many cupboards for the cover of this book. Also, to the entire Independent Thinking family, especially those who planned or took part in Thinking Saturdays. Those days gave me permission to be a learning geek and gave me a learning family with whom to share that experience.

Thank you to the wonderful team at Vision for Education, especially Liam, who inspired me to join the team through Haribo and Diet Coke, as well as Gareth and Paul for placing me in schools that helped me to reflect on teaching from an entirely new angle.

Also, thank you to my friends who 'believe' in my unorthodox ways and encourage my unusual journeys. Special thanks to Marsha Costigan for the cups of tea and motivating conversations in Dream Corner, and Isabella Wallace for her generosity, kindness and book recommendations which keep me always moving forward.

Finally, a huge thank you to my family for being there for me, no matter how stressful the writing became. To Tony, my husband, without whom I would starve both physically and intellectually. To my children who have embraced the dysfunction and keep me going through encouragement. To my brother for our joint dreams that keep me smiling. To my mam, Trish, who is a rock in any storm, and to Nana Ellen – legend.

CONTENTS

INTRODUCTION

> View the cupboard as a metaphor for self-blindness. It is an affliction that affects so many and can be crippling to personal progress. Whether you are a student who blames their bad education on their teachers or a teacher who can't control behaviour but never looks at their own, self-blindness can hold us all back.

People watching

It was my first day as a classroom assistant. Just 21 years old and straight from university, I was petrified! At five feet two inches tall, many students in this secondary school were already taller than me. I felt intimidated by the prospect of secondary students and intellectually inferior to the teachers. Having just completed an English degree, I had no clue what I was expected to do in this unfamiliar setting – unaware of my purpose and blind to my potential.

My first day was an INSET, which is the day (I quickly found out) when classroom assistants drink coffee and clean out cupboards. We were segregated from the teachers who, I could only assume, were being taught the magic of education in a hall somewhere else. My timetable wasn't ready but they assured me this was 'normal'. I was in no way prepared for classes of teenagers or terrifyingly professional teachers. My first day had left me even more unsure of what I was supposed to do as part of my new role, but the cupboards were sparkling!

When school really started, I was assigned to class 9Z3. My first lesson was English: I knew this subject! I had a degree in this subject! Hopefully, this would magically make me useful when the lesson began. I needn't have worried. As I arrived, the teacher gave me a look that screamed, 'Know your place!' Classroom assistants were not welcome in this room. Not only had this teacher undergone the magical INSET workshops that I was unworthy of, but she had been teaching for over twenty years and certainly didn't need my help. I was put in the cupboard.

I'm not talking about a metaphorical cupboard (yet). I was told that I should work in an actual cupboard, tucked away at the side of the classroom. Work? On what? Apart from following 9Z3 around the school, I didn't have any 'work' to do.

The Z in the class code was no accident. They were viewed by all as the bottom of the barrel. These kids were not expected to achieve. They were expected to be a pain in the arse. I wasn't earning much, but surely I was supposed to do more for my pittance than sit in a cupboard? Surely these Z-listers could use some support, right? But I knew better than to go against the experience of a well-established teacher. I took my seat in the cupboard and prepared to … well … sit.

> How often have you done something you know to be wrong but someone in charge told you to do it, so you did? Why? Do you lack confidence? Why?
>
> Check out the Milgram Experiment for some interesting further reading on this topic.[1]

It really wasn't that long since I had been sitting in the classroom myself, and college and university had not felt much different from school for me. They were institutions that I fell into; they were not well-thought-out stepping stones to my own success. There were teachers and lecturers who knew it all, and then there was me regurgitating what they said without much of a clue why. In my new cupboard, there was a gap in the door just wide enough to witness the lessons. I could picture myself sitting back in that classroom, as bored then as I was now. The lessons would go over my head as I stared out of the window and daydreamed about anything other than

---

1   See https://www.simplypsychology.org/milgram.html.

learning. Had I landed a job that took me right back to the place I had been so desperate to get away from?

The more I observed, the more I began to see. It was like watching a repeat of some old TV programme – the same lesson, the same behaviours from both the teacher and students. Like a fly on the wall, I became a teacher in training *from a cupboard*. My self-blindness had kept me from challenging the authority of the teacher. I knew it was wrong to be relegated to a cupboard, but in I went nevertheless. I couldn't see myself as anything other than subordinate. The cupboard would become a cure for self-blindness (although it is an ongoing regime of observation and reflection that keeps it at bay). I began to write down what I saw. As I travelled around the school with my Z-listers, I continued my observations, even in those classes where I was allowed to participate.

The titles of the chapters in this book are direct quotations from my observations in education. I've witnessed adults being hideous to children and expecting respect for their domineering behaviour. From my vantage point, the frustrations of teachers were obvious, but so were the mistakes they were making in the way they communicated with learners. Many students didn't give their teachers a chance and, time after time, perfectly good lessons were ruined out of childishness (and not just the kids'). The perspectives of both teacher and students were opened up to me.

Your problems are your problems

As you read through this book, I'm sure you will have problems in mind that you would like to solve. Some concerns already exist, some will bubble up and more will be waiting to appear as the years go by and the book gathers dust on your bookshelf. This truth is not stated to depress you; rather to remind you of reality.

Problems are part of life and certainly a frequent part of the life of a teacher. Perhaps there is a specific difficulty in your mind now? Picture that child, that manager, that class, that situation which is filling you with fear, loathing, frustration, hopelessness. Are you hoping that the solution will be found within these pages? I hope so too!

This book is filled with observations from my many varied experiences in education, alongside examples and practical strategies. However, without your commitment to connect the content to your context – and your belief in yourself as being instrumental in creating a solution – you will be in danger of falling at the first hurdle on the get-out clause of 'That won't work for me!' Know that this is just an excuse. The problem with excuses is that they make teachers feel justified in avoiding action, but they don't solve anything. Action is the only way you will move forward.

Take action before you read on. To complete this task, you will need:

+ Something to represent a target.

+ A timer.

+ Some sheets of scrap paper.

Go and get these things now. Set up your target on the other side of the room (or across the swimming pool if this is holiday reading!). You don't need to do this alone. If you have other people around you, make this a team challenge. The target could be a sheet of paper stuck to the wall; a bucket or a cardboard box would be even better. If you have a bigger space to play with, you might want to set up a line as your target to cross.

Don't read past this page until you have given this a go.

+ Set your timer for one minute.

+ When the timer starts, you have one minute to get as many paper aeroplanes made and across to your target as possible.

+ Stop when the time is up.

+ Once you've finished you can turn the page ...

A bike helmet did the trick when I challenged my husband with this task. He managed to get one plane on target.

He wasn't too impressed when I beat him a moment later using a little creativity!

Did you assume that a paper aeroplane needed to look like an actual aeroplane? Did you believe this task was so simple that there was no room for some creative thinking? Did you let the voice in your head tell you that you couldn't do this because you're no good at making/throwing/aiming? Or worse, did you just turn the page and hope that someone else had solved the problem for you? Perhaps you saw straight through my suggestion and created a solution that was much more likely to be successful? Good for you! You are already ready for this book.

This is a fun icebreaker task, usually best done in small groups.[2] No matter who I've played this game with in the past, much of the minute is always spent teaching each other how to make paper aeroplanes. Well-made planes may fly but very few hit the target. Successful players don't stick rigidly to the rules; they see that there is always space for a little imagination and that a paper plane could take any shape. It is quicker to crumple up balls of paper, which are also more likely to go further than a poorly made plane.

This task is a metaphor for the problems we all face in daily life. When a problem pops up, we often stick to the rules and solutions we already know. We focus on our lack of time and do things as they have been done by others in the past. Your teacher gremlin starts talking you down or holding you back from being proactive. It tells you, 'You're a fraud.' When a nightmare group, an inspection or a problem student comes along, it tells you, 'You're a lousy teacher – give up.' So we stop trying. We can't solve this one by crumpling up a sheet of paper, but it can be remedied by taking creative action.

If you listen to the gremlin, you will do nothing and hope that someone in charge will do all of the thinking for you. In that way, you get to sit in the staffroom and moan about what is going wrong without ever lifting a finger to put it right. However much you do this, the problems won't go away. Creativity can be blocked by being too serious, listening to your teacher gremlin without questioning it, sticking rigidly to the rules, reproaching yourself for your shortcomings, blaming circumstances or other people and avoiding risk. Now is the time to ban these blockers of creativity! Wake up to the insane voice of your teacher gremlin, take action and embrace being a creative problem solver!

How many problems have you heard being discussed in your staffroom this week? You can stop counting now. Did you pick up on problems with the way children are assessed, behaviour issues, inspections, professional development, work–life balance, new initiatives that not only don't work but make the job a

---

2   For more icebreakers like this see Edie West, *201 Icebreakers: Group Mixers, Warm Ups, Energisers and Playful Activities* (New York: McGraw-Hill, 1997).

lot harder? Even if all the current education problems have been solved by the time you read this, more would surface to take their place.

Problems are not the problem; excuses are.

The chapters in this book include real-life experiences to make you think, as well as practical solutions to some common problems. Hopefully, these ideas, methods and resources will give you the power and courage to act and find your own solutions. Remember, a paper plane can take any shape and your problems don't have only one answer. They have many, and it's *your* creativity that is going to be needed to find them. I found a variety of ways of dealing with the problems I witnessed from the cupboard, so let me now support you as you take action to change the lives of those you teach.

My experiences in education vary widely. As the book progresses, you will find yourself looking through various lenses, not always in the order that you might expect. As a classroom assistant, I was able to observe what did and didn't work. As a project coordinator, I was able to work with learning mentors, classroom teachers and outside providers. I have been a classroom teacher, a supply teacher, a head of department, an advanced skills teacher, a teaching and learning leader and a teaching consultant, and not strictly in that order. Life is not a straight line when you are investigating education. A week in my working life can go from consulting in an international private

> What are your current problems?
>
> What are you hoping to solve?

school to teaching a low-attaining group as a supply teacher. I use each role in which I find myself to further my understanding of education and how to get it right. I believe that if we are to support colleagues and students well, we need to be able to view things from their perspective.

Part I

THE VIEW FROM THE
CUPBOARD: STUDENTS

Chapter 1

GET SOME PERSPECTIVE!

Student's perspective

As I sat in my cupboard one day, a teacher took a child aside during a lesson to discuss unfinished coursework. The student had been in the learning mentor's office earlier that day, beside herself in panic, crying and looking for help. Her parents had just separated and she was unsure where she was going home to that night as both parents wanted custody. Home wasn't the easiest place to do coursework and she had arranged to have time out of another lesson to try to get her mind on her work. This teacher either didn't know any of this or didn't care, and quickly launched into a verbal assault. I heard and saw it all. The class did too.

Imagine the high-pitched, shaking voice of someone who has lost their composure as you read this:

> What's wrong with you? I'll tell you what, you're lazy! Why should I have to teach you? Why should I have to spend every night awake worrying about making sure you get a good education when you don't care yourself? Do you know the level of effort I go to for you? You deserve to fail this subject. Don't you know that this is such an important subject, if you do fail, you will fail in life?

Inspiring, right? Did her admonishment work? No. The child never came back into lessons after that day. It was almost exam season and the school wrote her off, allowing her an early 'study' leave.

Have you ever taken your emotions out on a child? Why?

Try a daily mantra when working with frustrating children: *no emotional response*!

Teacher's perspective

Despite the teacher seeming to be the villain here, she was trying to do the best thing by the child. She wanted her to hand in coursework. Doing so would have improved her chances of passing a subject that is required to get onto many college courses. Instead, she succeeded in turning her off school. This same teacher had been pretending to have hay fever for the past week. I saw her crying in her classroom, but her eyes were not red from pollen. She had been the talk of the staffroom because of her unsatisfactory results. Everyone knew her teaching was substandard. She was always given the bottom sets to avoid her failing any of the 'important' students. She was on a programme designed to manage teachers who did not deliver out of the profession.

This teacher did not want the student to fail, but she did create the failure. The child was finding her world unbearable. The teacher was adding to that pressure because the pressure she was under herself was bubbling over into the classroom. Communication and mutual understanding was lacking. Neither party could step back and look from the perspective of the other. If only they could have stepped inside the cupboard to view the reality of their situation. Both teacher and student were blind to themselves and to each other.

As time went on, I witnessed senior leaders making fools of themselves by following a 'how to' guide to management, teachers in tears over poor behaviour, teachers unable to cope with heavy workloads, managers unable to empathise with those beneath them. Why couldn't they see that what was going wrong was caused by their own behaviour? Their teacher gremlins were creating this insanity,

> How often do you stop to look from the perspective of others?
>
> Do your moods follow you into work?

and problems were being perpetuated rather than solved. My vantage point gave me an enlightening view. Perhaps everyone should spend a year in a cupboard in order to witness the craziness that people inflict on each other every day! By staying in the same old rut, these teachers had become blind to themselves, to their potential and to their impact on others.

It wasn't all bad. I witnessed the most amazing teachers taking 'difficult' children on learning journeys too. Maths was always alien to me and yet the maths teacher got down to the level of his students (my level), and I learned more in that classroom than I did in five years at my own secondary school. I got to spy on what worked and what didn't, and I had the time to process this and apply it to my own development. The power of observation began to shape my understanding of education practices. My cupboard observations continued, even when I escaped to a new school. I remained hooked on understanding what was going wrong for students (like me), what was getting in the way of success for teachers and leaders, and what we could do to put it right.

Stop, look and listen

Before we move on to the next section, a quick reality check is necessary. As teachers, we deal with human beings – students, parents and colleagues. People don't always respond in the way we hope or expect them to. Approaching any difficult situation requires care and a recognition of the humanity in the other person. I often use mantras to avoid my emotions clouding my conversations. Remember this and create your own with this understanding in mind.

Inventing on-the-spot 'cupboard time' for yourself can improve your relationships and your ability to deal with emotional situations in the moment. Gaining the perspective of those around you requires you to put your ego, emotions and gremlins to one side. The teacher I just described acted in the moment. No breaths were taken, with the result being detrimental to the future of the child. Could she have stopped? Could she have questioned? Could she have taken a route that kept the student in school?

The gremlin got the better of that teacher. She wanted to assert her power to show the child exactly how angry her actions had made her. The gremlin in your head will get in the way of positive outcomes during emotional exchanges too. 'Who does she think she is?' 'Why doesn't he understand what I'm trying to say?' 'How dare they …?' We can't control the actions or words of others, but we are responsible for our own. We need to know when to stop and assess what is really going on.

You can get into your metaphorical cupboard at any time – when a student is being difficult, when a colleague is stepping on your toes, when a leader is being overbearing. These are the times when you should seek out the other person's perspective. Observe the voices in your own mind and be aware of your initial reaction, but try to not act on it. What is the bigger picture? Why is the other person acting like that? What is their motivation? What could be done to create positive outcomes for all? Fight your inner self-preserving anger and bring yourself into the reality of the moment.

We can't jump inside the minds of those around us. If we could, we would either all get along a whole lot better or we would never talk to anyone again! In the 2000 film *What Women Want*, Mel Gibson is granted the power to see inside the minds of women. Selfishly, he uses this power to further his love life and career rather than improve his relationships. What would you use the power for? In fact, you *can* have that power – not in a supernatural mind-reading way, but by better understanding others and their situation. You can only try to understand other people's point of view by looking at the clues they are giving you. Whoever presents you with a difficult conversation, an emotional exchange or an infuriating demand will become the subject of your cupboard time.

Listening is easier said than done. To listen, you must empty your mind, be present and hear what words are being said, as well as observe how they are being said. What is being verbalised can give you clues to the deeper issues within, but so can observing more subtle cues like body language and facial expression. If you are listening but waiting to get your point across, you may miss the subtleties that non-verbal cues are giving away. A raised eyebrow, tightening of the lips, movement of the body away/towards you – the shoulders, arms, legs and feet all give clues to the inner realities of that person.[1] If there is conflict between you and another person, careful listening is far more likely to resolve that conflict than bulldozing them with your own opinions. Even if you get your perspective across and get them to change theirs, you have likely made an enemy for life.

Questioning is an essential element of listening. Careful questioning can help us to find out why the other person feels/thinks/acts in the way they do. As you will see in the examples below, we often make up reasons for ourselves to explain why our students are behaving in negative ways, rather than questioning them further to find out the actual truth.

How many of these 'You … because …' statements, heard in classrooms up and down the country, have you been guilty of uttering in the past?

> You are always fidgeting because you're not interested in my subject.

> You never behave because you're showing off!

> You never listen because you're too interested in yourself.

> You can't sit still because you're distracted.

In each of these statements an assumption has been made: our perspective is the only one to be considered, and nothing has been achieved in the exchange. Most teachers want children to be instantly sorry about their poor behaviour – 'Yes Miss, sorry Miss' is the acceptable response. Once we have asserted our authority we can move back to the teaching. What has the child learned from this – to accept adults as all-knowing beings who control with superior knowledge? Maybe. Think about the many situations in which believing that an adult is always right and never questioning their authority can be detrimental to a child's safety. Of course, manners and respect are important. But so is learning to look at yourself and regulate your behaviour – and that goes for both adults and children.

---

1   If you want to explore body language more deeply, an excellent resource is Joe Navarro and Marvin Karlins' *What Every Body is Saying: An Ex-FBI Agent's Guide to Speed-Reading People* (New York: HarperCollins, 2008).

Imagine if the teacher had used cupboard time and questions instead of accusatory statements:

- *Statement of fact*: You weren't listening to me just now. Is that right?

- *Response*: Yes, Miss.

- *Question*: Why? What was going on in your mind?

- *Response*: When you mentioned X it reminded me of Y and my mind wandered.

- *Move forward*: That happens to me sometimes too. In class, you will do better if you can recognise those times when your mind wanders. Do you think we could work on getting that right together?

- *Response*: Yes, Miss.

This is an example of the exchange in a perfect world. The mantra 'Stop, look and listen' is in play here and the bullet points – statement of fact, response, question, response, move forward, response – provide a useful scaffold. But, as I've already mentioned, you are dealing with human beings and their responses can't be predicted. The only thing you have control over is yourself. The main thing is not to react emotionally. Keep the conversation focused and clear by using the mantra and the scaffold. Moving forward, not punishment, is your end game. Model the behaviour you want to nurture in the children you teach.

The same technique works with colleagues too:

- *Statement of fact*: Your books were not marked this week. Is that right?

  As the person in charge of monitoring this situation, you have to ensure that things are getting done. You don't have to assert your power over that person in a negative way. Use questioning to find a way forward together.

- *Response*: Yes but …

  There is likely to be a defensive response to an issue like this. They may go on the attack, but you can turn the negative into a positive if you choose the right question as a follow-up. You may hear: 'My child was sick.' There were just too many other things that needed to be done first.' 'I left them on a bus and only got the chance to pick them up from the depot yesterday!' Whatever the response, listen and form a question that can take you both forward.

* *Question*: Is there anything I can do to help?

* *Response*: Errrm …

This might take them a moment if they are more used to being put in their place than offered support. Have some ideas ready to help them out. You are not demanding that the books are marked right away. You are recognising an issue and supporting that colleague in finding a solution. You are not making an enemy – you are creating a collaborative environment where things get done.

Why bother?

Do you think the exchange between the teacher and student would result in the child listening intently to each and every word the teacher said for evermore? Do you listen to each and every word your leaders say to you in briefings? Does your mind wander? Are you, as an adult, a perfect product? Of course not. But by creating on-the-spot cupboard time in moments of heightened emotion, we can work together towards a cooperative learning environment, rather than leading mini dictatorships that could be overthrown at the whim of *that* child.

Teaching children metacognition is a more realistic pursuit than teaching them perfection. The Education Endowment Foundation have recognised this as one of the most effective ways to raise attainment.[2] Teaching students that no one is perfect and that our minds do wander – but that we are in control of our thoughts and actions – can help them to make better choices

---

2   See https://educationendowmentfoundation.org.uk/evidence-summaries/teaching-learning-toolkit/meta-cognition-and-self-regulation/.

and feel better about themselves when they do make mistakes. For teachers, understanding our own thought processes can help us to be more mindful in the classroom, and to approach difficult situations with tact and humanity.

By questioning students, we can find out more about the reality of their situation. We can model empathy by demonstrating that we are human too. It is not just our subject knowledge that rubs off on them. Our attitudes and behaviour are on show for all to see and copy. What impact might it have on student behaviour if we play the part of a strict authoritarian, demand perfection and don't show our human side? Will they grow up to behave in the same way with their own children? Will they look at themselves as imperfect in a world that demands perfection? Will they feel that they will never be what we want them to be and simply give up? There is always another way. Children are adults in training. Let's show them the power of being in control.

When working with colleagues, recognising their situation and pausing before we take action will win us their respect and create a cooperative workplace. Too many schools are run on fear. Conversations in the staffroom revolve around how the leaders are ineffective, yet nobody dares to tell them what the problems are. In schools where dialogue trumps accusations, a community of support can evolve. Problems can be resolved as people talk openly and support each other to solve them. I know which school I would rather work in.

Try this!

Statement of fact: Don't put any emotion into this. Be clear on the issue and make sure that what is being discussed is unambiguous to both of you. What action/lack of action has led to this discussion?

Response: Do you both agree? If not, don't argue and demand. Find out their point of view and settle on an agreed reason for the discussion. If you ask, 'You were talking during my explanation. Is that right?' and they answer, 'No,' your next question would be, 'What do you think happened?' Usually, they will respond with, 'Well, G whispered and so I was just replying,' or something similar, which means they were doing exactly what you suggested but just not quite how you put it. That's okay. You can now use what they have said to reframe the statement of fact: 'You were answering another student while I was explaining something. Is that right?' It is right because you have used their own words. You are seeing the situation from their point of view. It is very easy to slip into smart-arse mode here, but the purpose is to agree on the reason for your discussion. This response needs to be mutually agreed in order for you both to move on. Remember that you can't predict or control the responses of others, but you can listen carefully in order to understand and you can stay in control of the direction of the conversation.

Question: This should help you to listen to their point of view so that you can frame a moving forward idea that works for you both. Do they often do that? Are they struggling with where they are sitting? Why do they think this happened? You want the other person to think through their own thought processes; you don't want them quaking in fear. You want them to see that they can move forward from their current position into one that works for you both.

Response: Whatever happens here you need to *listen*. Empty your mind, be present and pay attention. What solutions can you create from their current position? What tools can you give them to avoid future issues? What situation are they in that you can help them to get out of? How can you help each other to move forward?

Move forward: Be clear on the plan and ask them to agree to it. Once the plan is in place, don't let the initial behaviour interfere with your thoughts or feelings towards them. Move ahead and praise the improvement as it comes.

Of course, you will encounter extreme situations. There will be times when the other person won't respond positively to anything you say. There will be stubborn people and those who bulldoze you with their emotions. When those individuals pop up, try to stay true to a calmer you. Get into your cupboard and observe what is happening. Try to understand the reasons behind their melodrama, but never let yourself join in just to feed the teacher gremlin.

Chapter 2

IT'S ALL THEIR FAULT!

> We are all selfish. Recognising this is the first step to
> overcoming egotism as a barrier to self-improvement.
> Do you want to be a more switched on, reflective teacher?
> Do you dare blame yourself when things go wrong?

Teacher versus student

You are the most important person in your life. You can't help feeling that – it's normal. You are stuck behind your own eyes and you've only got access to your own feelings. However, when your own self-importance or emotions get in the way of clarity, it becomes a problem in teaching (and life). I have witnessed self-blindness on many occasions through the crack in the cupboard door.

When you hear a teacher desperately throwing out questions, you know they have stopped looking at themselves and are blaming the child:

Teacher: Why won't you listen?

Student: Coz you're shouting and haven't tried to get to know me.

Teacher: What's your problem?

Student: Would you like a list, Miss?

Teacher: Why won't you just behave?

Student: Coz it's way easier to take the piss out of you.

I've seen adults break down because of poor behaviour and observed children thrive on their pain.

The class that wouldn't behave

As I explained in the introduction, during my first year in education, my role was to support class 9Z3 across the whole curriculum. Although I did not have the confidence to step in and challenge some of the dreadful experiences they encountered, these observations have stayed with me throughout my career and are often the driving force behind my search for solutions. One such observation happened in the last lesson on a Tuesday afternoon when 9Z3 found themselves in geography.

This day of the week was unlike the rest: lunch was followed by the final lesson of the day. At 2pm the bell would ring and the school day was over for the students. At 2pm, the teachers had professional development time (also known as 'ranting about 9Z3 time' for this particular geography teacher). Something about this unusual timetabling sent the class wild. 'If you could just listen …' the teacher would wail endlessly in her high-pitched voice, but to no avail. The students had no intention of listening, and as an inexperienced observer I was of no help either.

It felt as if my role was to keep the teacher from losing her mind; at least she had another adult in the room to roll her eyes at and ask for reassurance: 'It's not me, is it? It's them.' The whole year went on like this. Students would be sent out, detentions dispensed, shouting lavished on them like sun cream in the Sahara. Nothing changed. Nothing improved. Tuesday afternoons were a battle that only the students seemed to enjoy.

At this point, I had never taught, but I knew there had to be more to this than a crazy class or an ineffectual teacher. I had watched 9Z3 behave well in other subjects. I knew they had it in them. Over time, I worked on solutions for classes just like this one. No two situations are the same but these kinds of classes exist in schools all over the world.

Although this book contains many of the common problems I have witnessed in education, this is not a book about problems. It is a book about overcoming any obstacle, no matter how tricky it may seem when you are in the thick of it.

In this section I am going to introduce a method of problem solving which I will revisit throughout the book. It is a method that I have returned to time and again because it gets me started on solving a problem as soon as it arises. First, I *observe the problem* in depth; next, I use my observations to *create a solution*, complete with a question that I want to answer; then I *test that solution* as I am practising; and, finally, I *review my findings* to determine the next steps.

I have used this process to solve issues with poor student behaviour, to challenge high attainers, to deal with teachers who have lost their love for the practice and in many more testing situations. I believe that any problem can be solved if we adopt the right attitude and take action.

Observation

One problem that I came across during my time as a leader was that some teachers felt that my position in the school meant that the strategies I used would not work for them. Many years after my first experiences with 9Z3, by now an advanced skills teaching and learning leader, I was told by a colleague that my methods only worked because I was well respected: teachers and students alike looked up to me. Apparently, I could walk into a classroom backwards and demand they all screech like chimps for an hour and it would work because of who I was in the school! Rather than dismissing this as the teacher's problem, I decided to look at the issue in more depth.

This colleague (and many others) saw me as someone in charge who should be solving their problems for them. From my perspective, I wanted to use my knowledge and expertise to crack problems with behaviour, engagement, challenge, support and more. My role as a learning leader, which gave me access to the whole staff for professional development sessions and pedagogical knowledge sharing, should have been enough for me to do just that. However, because I was not in *exactly* the same position as this person, they did not believe in my solutions. In fact, they saw these solutions as yet another problem they had no power to solve.

In fact, my leadership position and knowledge were getting in the way of this teacher's confidence in me. In other words, my colleague's perspective was the problem I needed to solve. Observing this, I came up with a solution-focused question: *do the methods I employ work for me when I am not a well-known leader of learning?* From that question came the solution.

Solution

If I wanted to give advice to struggling teachers, I realised that I would need to explore problems from their point of view – and from this realisation my solution was born: I became a supply teacher. My intention was to place myself in a position where I was unknown and where I would have no power. In that way, I could truly investigate my question. Do my methods really work when I am not an established teacher?

It was too late to turn back – I was about to find out! As a supply teacher for the first time, I found myself standing in front of a new class, when a teacher shouted over her shoulder to a colleague, 'I'll be with you soon. I have to sort out all the bloomin' supply teachers first.' Nice! The attitude demonstrated a lack of respect, as if even the teachers wanted to put 'kick me' signs on my back as I walked down the corridor. This was the perfect place to test out my solution.

Testing the solution

Not everything I tried worked perfectly (as you will see below). My reflective attitude had to endure through some very tough situations. Whether I was exploring how to establish respect quickly or trying out a new resource to accelerate learning, I had to reflect constantly throughout the process. Returning to my solution-focused question helped me to stay dedicated.

> Who do you blame when things go wrong? Yourself or everyone else? Why?
>
> Do you ever see situations as hopeless and avoid doing anything about them, knowing that in a year's time they will be someone else's problem? Why?
>
> Do you believe that every problem can be solved if you look carefully from all perspectives?

Review

For smaller investigations, I would review each solution after I had tested it, asking myself: did that work? How? Why? What did I learn? If it didn't work, why not? What haven't I tried yet? What do I need to adapt? What are my next steps as a result of what I have learned?

The review stage helps to remind us that this is an ongoing process. We are looking for next steps through the questions we ask. Teaching can be a crazy job, and it is easy to get down about bad days (and there were many of them, believe me). But the bad days are a learning resource too, and reassessing our ideas can lead to a richer understanding of educational problems.

So, did the methods work for me when I was not a well-known leader of learning? Sometimes yes and sometimes no. I found that I had to be far more reflective, focused and creative as a supply teacher. The colleague who had doubted me at the start of the process had presented me with a challenge. Entering into a problem-solving process, rather than dismissing their point of view, led to a far better understanding of all my colleagues' perspectives.

The next time you catch yourself complaining about a problem (we all do it!), why not challenge yourself to solve it? Problems will always exist, but how you deal with those problems can make a huge difference to your practice. Use the table below to begin forming solutions to a problem you want to solve.

What question do you want to ask about the problem?	
Observe the problem from all perspectives. What is happening right now?	
Come up with a solution. It helps if you have a solution-focused question with which to train your efforts. What will you do to attempt to solve your problem? What do you hope will happen as a result of your solution?	
Test the solution. Put your solution into practice and observe what happens.	
Review your results. Return to your question. Did you answer it? Did your solution work? If not, why not? What are your next steps?	

Solving the problem of poor student behaviour

When poor student behaviour is making life a misery, it is easy to slip back into a 'That won't work for me' mindset. That's because our behaviour is having an effect on our emotions. It happens to us all. This emotional response can impede the problem-solving process as we struggle to regain control.

I faced this problem during one particularly tricky supply placement which I describe below. This example goes into more depth on the *observation*, *solution*, *testing the solution* and *review* process to show that it is possible to control your emotions and come up with a solution.

I am a confident supply teacher and I always plan my lessons with the learners in mind. However, this didn't help me one bit when my new Year 10 class arrived. They had me pegged for fresh meat, and it had been only a matter of weeks since the last supply teacher had refused to return. The students worked together as a pack, refused to listen, fought among themselves, threw equipment around the room and left the lesson believing they had thoroughly crushed my spirit. They had. I was so distraught about the experience that I was blind to their perspective and could only feel my own. Everything I could usually do so well had been ruined by these teenagers; my confidence was shattered and (for a short time) it felt that I would never be able to gain control.

There was an obvious problem with student behaviour that needed to be addressed. I should have been starting the observation process, but my emotions were getting in the way. Before I could observe the problem, I first had to cultivate the right mindset.

For some time after the horrendous lesson, I had immobilising feelings of despair. You know the feeling – when it doesn't matter what people say or do to try to make you feel better. When you can't see past the end of your nose because your judgement is clouded by the painful feelings caused by the situation. It is too raw. 'Why don't you try …?' my husband would helpfully suggest. But before he could even finish his sentence, I had ended it for him with a death stare that told him his suggestions were not welcome. My emotions were running high, and if left there they would prevent me from coming up with a creative solution. Before I could observe the problem carefully, I had to regain control.

Quietening our emotions is not an easy task, so don't try to jump straight in while you are in a heightened state following a poor lesson. The following process helped me to regain clarity and eventually discover the solution to my class' problem. It was a bit like active meditation.

> Do you hold on to the things that go wrong more than the things that go right? Why?
>
> How often can you find solutions while in a rubbish mood?

Step 1: Take time to regain control

Give yourself some time to calm down because negative feelings can have a detrimental effect on the journey towards a positive outcome. It almost seems unnecessary to point out that it takes time, but I constantly have to remind myself of this so I am offering it as advice to you too. I walked away from my appalling class feeling like a fraud. Those familiar words, 'That won't work for me', rang loudly in my ears. Imagine my drooping gait and my nosedive onto the sofa to wallow in self-pity. I could have remained in this state – it wasn't easy to talk myself out of it – but I repeated the mantra 'take time' over and over to remind myself that this was just the start and that a solution would come.

Step 2: Refocus on the positive

As we've already seen, the cupboard is a metaphor for removing ourselves from the situation and seeing the world from a different place. When we are stressed out, we need to re-engage with the positive. The critical voice inside our head can and will take over if we let it. Take control! This is not the time for thinking about what went wrong or desperately searching for an answer. Stop the endless self-criticism, 'I should have …' 'If only …' 'I'm rubbish because …' and begin to nurture a more constructive inner voice. Start by observing yourself in the best class you have ever taught. Look through their eyes and see what they see. You *are* the teacher you want to be! This is not a narcissistic exercise, and you should not feel guilty about accessing pleasing memories about yourself.

Here is the scenario that ran through my mind when I was on my mission to realign with my positive, problem-solving self: as Year 7 calmly enter the room, I see my smile. They know I am pleased to see them. Each child gets a 'Good morning' and there is lots of excited, 'What are we doing today, Miss?' chatter. They are clearly intrigued by the image on the board of an old lady sitting in the gutter and begin to discuss their starting question. They know when to listen and that listening is worthwhile because the next step always takes them on a learning journey. I begin to relax as I see the teacher they see, and know that it is the best version of me – the version I want all of my classes to get to know.

> How do you make sure that your emotions don't take over?

You may notice that this cupboard reflection of myself was not immediately helpful in finding a solution. The aim was to refocus my energy towards the positive, to observe what had gone down well in other groups and to quieten that nagging inner critic. The time you spend in positive reflection should lift your energy and make you feel bloody good before you start to tackle the problem. However, if you find yourself saying, 'Screw them – I'm an awesome teacher. Those little fools are the problem, not me,' you are not yet in the right place to find solutions.

What worked well in other classes is unlikely to work with your problem group because, the chances are, you've tried it already. I had made an effort to greet them all nicely, to open with an intriguing image and to plan the learning process perfectly, and it hadn't worked. Now that you are calm and in control, it is time to search for solutions that *will* work.

Step 3: Creating solution-focused questions

A solution-focused question can help us to come up with ideas and reflect on our process. When we first come out of a terrible lesson, we may find ourselves asking, 'Why won't they just behave?' or 'Why can't I teach them?' We are asking the wrong questions!

We have identified a problem – poor student behaviour – but our questions lead to excuses, not solutions. These kinds of questions only result in an avalanche of reasons that continue to support the inference that they are unteachable and that you will never enjoy teaching them. For example, if we ask, 'Why won't the class behave?' our teacher gremlin will ping back many justifications: you are a rubbish teacher; they come from bad families; they are terrible with everyone; they are robots programmed to find your weakness and exploit it. These explanations may feel real, but they are unhelpful when it comes to moving forward. They are keeping us locked in battle without a solution.

Instead, we can try asking, 'How can I manage this class to support them in behaving well?' or 'How can I adapt so that we can all enjoy this lesson and they can learn?' By reframing these questions in this way, we are forcing ourselves to look for solutions rather than validating unhealthy feelings. (If you find yourself yelling these reframed questions in an angry voice, then the chances are you are still focused on the negative. Return to step 2!) Reframing questions is part of our observation of the problem.

If the question does not come easily, we can try using the Question Formulation Technique (QFT) which was developed by the Right Question Institute.[1]

---

1   See rightquestion.org.

It is widely used to encourage students to ask their own questions, but we are going to use it here to develop our solution-focused question.

First, write down every question that pops into your mind regarding the current issue. Every question has the potential to become a solution, so don't hold back – ask them all. A key ring of question stems, which I use when getting students to generate questions about a topic, comes in handy for this process (there are some Question Stem Cards in the Resource Cupboard at the back of the book). Don't worry about the question being silly; don't worry whether it even makes sense. This is a brain dump and will be sorted out later.

For my difficult class I wrote down dozens of questions, including:

+ What's going on?

+ Why does X never listen?

+ What happened when I spoke to the whole class?

+ At what point did it all go wrong?

+ Was there a point when I was in control?

+ Was there a point when I lost control?

+ Who is instigating the bad behaviour?

+ Why are they not engaging?

+ How do they see me?

+ How do they react to consequences?

+ Do they respond well to other teachers?

+ What is their past experience in this particular lesson?

+ What was I doing at distinct points in the lesson that I can adapt or change to create different outcomes?

Some of the these questions were helpful, some were unhelpful. That's okay. They were all a starting point.

When you feel that you have all the questions you can muster, reframe any unhelpful ones into solution-finding questions. For example, 'Why does X never listen?' could create a whole host of reasons without solutions, but 'What could gain and retain X's attention?' is more constructive. 'Why are they not engaging?' could become 'What methods have I already tried to engage them with, and what other methods could be used?'

Now that you have removed the emotions that were blocking your problem-solving capability and created a clear, solution-focused question to investigate, you are back to the problem-solving steps: *observe* the problem from all perspectives (what is really going on?), use your observations to *find a solution*, *test the solution* by putting it into action and *review* the effect of your solution to create the next steps.

Let's continue the journey with my seemingly uncontrollable class as I put the problem-solving steps into action.

Observation

By using the above steps, I moved away from my overwrought emotions and created one solution-focused question: *how can I create an environment that we all look forward to being in?* To answer this question, I first had to observe everything that was happening from all perspectives.

In myself, I saw an overly confident teacher who thought she had all the answers to behaviour management. But she didn't know the students in front of her, she only thought she did. When the usual rules didn't work, she blamed the students and retreated into self-pity, rendering her unable to assess the situation properly. She was standing at the front of the class and barking to get attention. When she did not get that attention, she began to throw out consequences that had no impact on the students' behaviour. They knew the school better than she did, and they knew exactly how to avoid punishment.

Next, I saw students who had been subjected to supply teachers many times before. They knew that these half-teachers weren't held in high regard by anyone. Messing about gave the students a sense of satisfaction because they were gaining respect from their peers (a respect they did not crave from the face at the front of the room). They didn't want to get to know the teacher because so many supply teachers had given up on them before. They perceived there to be little or no consequences for their negative behaviour, so they felt reassured that they didn't need to listen or respond. They valued their own time but not their teacher's. They looked up to their head of year (he'd popped his head in and they'd had that irritating moment of good behaviour that had nothing to do with me).

By using this information, along with my solution-focused question, I began to generate ideas:

+ I could use the head of year as an ally.

+ I could make the classroom my environment by changing its appearance in a shocking way.

+ I could simplify the rules so that it would be impossible not to follow them.

+ I could create unbreakable consequences that would impinge on their time but also allow them to get to know me.

+ I could use my observations to create a very different lesson that would help us to bond before I started teaching them.

+ I had to remember to avoid reacting with my emotions.

Solution

I planned the next lesson meticulously, incorporating various elements that would help me to answer my question. I needed to:

+ Tackle the lack of respect for the rules by creating a simple rule that was unambiguous and had a clear consequence.

- Tackle the issue of ownership of the space by taking control of it.

- Tackle the issue of inappropriate speaking and lack of listening by teaching them to turn take and listen carefully.

- Tackle the issue of moving forward together.

With all of the above in place, I could organise a moving forward conference.

Testing the solution

As I taught the lesson, I tested my solutions for their ability to help me answer my question.

Tackling the lack of respect for the rules

I needed an immediate consequence for any poor behaviour so I could demonstrate that I meant what I said and gain authority. My intention was not to punish unnecessarily, but to get the students to understand that I should be respected as much as their head of year. The next lesson with the class was due to take place at the end of the school day. I enlisted the help of the head of year who called all the students' parents to ask them for their permission to keep their child behind for one hour if they did not follow my one rule (which I will come on to shortly).

Some parents were angry. How dare I suggest that their child would misbehave? He explained that this consequence would only affect those students who did not work within the rule. If their child could control their behaviour, there would be no reason to keep them behind. It's not that I thought a detention would teach them that I was boss; rather, I wanted the opportunity to talk one-on-one with any

> Do you judge teachers who need support from their colleagues as being weaker than you?

students who refused to take part in the 'moving forward' lesson that I had planned.

Tackling the issue of ownership of the space

As I reflected on the previous lesson, I realised that the students were faced with the familiar situation of an unfamiliar supply teacher trying to teach them. To move forward, I wanted them to feel that this situation was different, so I removed the tables and chairs from the room.

Tackling the issue of inappropriate speaking and lack of listening

As the students entered, they found me sitting on the floor facing a circle of papers with one simple rule written out clearly: 'Only the person holding the conch can speak.'

How often have you tried the same thing and expected different results?

The consequence for non-compliance was also clearly communicated: if they did not follow my single rule, they would remain behind after school for one hour. I invited the students to sit in the circle with me and, as I was holding the conch (a frisbee with the word 'conch' written on it!), I repeated the rule. The shock of such an unusual situation certainly had the desired effect. One by one, they came and sat in the circle. Nobody spoke as they waited to see what would happen.

The makeshift conch was symbolic of turn taking in our conversation. It gave the power to speak, but it also required others to listen before taking their turn. I explained the role of the conch in William Golding's *Lord of the Flies*, and how it relates to democracy. I also detailed why I felt the need to use one in the classroom. I then added some depth by including a brief introduction to Grice's maxims, which I would later use to help the students understand what a quality conversation should involve.[2] For example, we should always tell each other the truth, we should always show good manners (such as eye contact and back channelling) to show we are listening, we should not take over and we should relate what we say to what has just been said.

The class sat in silence throughout. It was the first time I had been able to speak to the group without being shouted down or laughed at for daring to try to teach. It was too early to congratulate myself (the shock could wear off at any moment), and I had to repeat 'no emotional response' in my mind to keep myself focused on the task. Remember that my question was not, 'How can I perfectly control this class?'; it was to find a solution that would be enjoyable for all. The control was necessary to begin the process of meaningful conversation.

Tackling the issue of moving forward together

Asking the right question, *how can I create an environment that we all look forward to being in?* had led me to this point. Now, asking the right questions

---

2   For more on Grice's maxims see Robert E. Frederking, Grice's Maxims: 'Do the Right Thing'. Presented at the Computational Implicature Workshop at the AAAI-96 Spring Symposium Series, Stanford University, 25–27 March 1996. Available at: http://www.cs.cmu.edu/afs/cs.cmu.edu/Web/People/ref/grice-final.pdf.

was going to enable all of us to achieve an answer. My purpose was not to get them to listen to me as their leader, but for us all to listen to each other – for me to get to know them and for them to get to know me. I set them a series of questions that started by looking back and then quickly moved to looking forward positively (see the Moving Forward Conference Cards in the Resource Cupboard). The big question at the heart of this discussion was: how can we create an environment that allows us to show respect towards each other, learn loads and enjoy Tuesday afternoons together?

+ Very little learning happened last lesson. What caused this and how did you feel?

+ What would have made things better last lesson?

+ What, from your perspective, makes a good lesson?

+ What would make you want to learn?

+ What rules would you like to put in place to make sure that our class is calm and productive?

+ What consequences should there be if anyone breaks our rules?

+ What questions do you have that may make a difference to our group?

I explained my feelings about the first question before I invited the students to join in. At first, there was a mutual awkwardness. My heartfelt description of how they had made me feel was in stark contrast to how they felt about it. As the conch was passed around, they explained that they were 'just messing about' or 'being daft'. They hadn't meant it personally.

Quickly leaving the negativity behind, the questions then began to focus on their likes and dislikes surrounding school. I posed the questions, offered them my thoughts and then passed the conch to the students waiting patiently to give their opinion. I asked them to record every idea so that we could use their suggestions to move forward. We discussed what they wanted from our lessons and what lessons they enjoyed most. Before long, we were laughing together. They were telling me stories about their favourite lessons and I piped up with some of mine. Who would have thought that this daffy supply teacher had created a 'wonderland' when reading Lewis Carroll or had dead bodies come to life to give everyone a fright during a topic on horror? Who would have thought that these uncontrollable children would have enjoyed lessons where they got to read out loud to the rest of the class or build rockets out of junk?

Gradually we got to know one another. Together we created a class manifesto that detailed a way forward for Tuesday afternoons so that it could become a lesson which we all looked forward to being in. The students each received a copy of the manifesto and agreed to abide by it, as it was created by them.

Year 10 Class Manifesto

Creating an environment that we look forward to being part of:

Listening skills. At times, the teacher will need to give direct instruction. This will be indicated by a countdown and a raised conch. Listen to the instructions. Raise your hand if you need to ask a question or make a point.

Behaviour for learning. We agreed that unacceptable behaviour will affect our learning. The teacher should not give consequences to the whole class, only to those displaying unacceptable behaviour. We agreed that unacceptable behaviour is: throwing things around, play fighting, swearing, bringing problems into the classroom, interrupting people when they are talking, refusing to listen, not trying with tasks and breaking equipment.

Teacher commitment. We want an environment in which we can learn lots and look forward to being in. The teacher has agreed to take into consideration what students enjoy doing when planning lessons. The following ideas were put forward:

- Prizes/rewards

- Sports

- Posters

- Read poems as a class

- Take turns reading

- Practical

- Out of the classroom

- Building models

- Act out poems

- School trips

- Fun

- Exciting poems

- Change the shape of the tables

- Discussions with the whole class

Note: The teacher will continue to take the above list into consideration when planning lessons, as long as students continue to play their part and take control of their own behaviour.

Signed _____

Review

In those first encounters, I had allowed my emotions to cloud the reality of the situation. Stepping back into the cupboard, I was able to revaluate and create a solution. Notice that the students had not asked for anything outlandish; their view of a good lesson did not differ that much from mine. Following the moving forward conference, the lessons continued to be successful as we had taken time out to get to know each other. They already knew what poor behaviour looked like and they had agreed as a group to avoid it in return for good teaching. It was also a fair deal from my perspective – that was all I had ever wanted from them and to provide for them.

Now, I regularly use the moving forward conference when starting new long-term placements or meeting a class for the first time. Why wait for the problem to start when I have developed a successful solution? If this way of working ever stops being effective, no worries, I simply have a new problem to solve.

Try this!

Use the table that follows to take action in changing how you approach difficult classes. Observe yourself during your worst and best classes. What language do you use to speak to them? When they ask you a question, how do you respond? When they are worried about their work, how do you react? What words do you use? Note down a selection of the most commonly used expressions from each class in the columns below. Filming yourself teaching is the best way to review your language use; however, you could also ask a colleague to observe you or just scribble down words as the lesson progresses or after it has finished.

Perhaps the language in each column is exactly the same. If this is the case, then there will be another solution to your problem, but it's not linguistic. I found that there was a difference between the language I used in different classes. The first column reminded me to use more supportive and less judgemental language with my worst classes. I later reflected that my change in language had changed their attitudes for the better. Try it out for yourself and see if it has a positive impact for you.

The language I use with my best class	The language I use with my worst class
Reflection: What effect did using your best class language have on your worst class?	

Everyone has bad days and not every lesson is perfect. Even the most experienced teachers can't pull off perfection 100% of the time. If my moving forward lesson had been unsuccessful, I would have repeated the process with the new data I'd gathered; not everything will work from the outset. The more time you spend examining yourself, your students and your colleagues from the perspective of the cupboard, the more accomplished you will become in your teaching practice.

Think back to the paper aeroplane task in the introduction. All you need is a little space, a change of perspective and some creativity, and you can solve most teaching problems. Of course, you always have the option of giving up, but that is not half as satisfying as finding a solution. Instead of saying, 'That won't work for me,' why not ask, 'How can I get that to work for me?' Try to have this question handy at all times because it's easy to forget and descend into the old ways – ways that don't work.

Chapter 3

THEY'LL NEVER LEARN!

> Everyone has problems. Some have it far harder than others.

Have you ever thought to yourself, 'If N isn't in today, my lesson will go well'? I've heard it frequently in staffrooms over coffee: 'I'm getting observed. I hope N is absent – she'll ruin everything!' I also know of teachers purposely removing specific students from their classroom during observed lessons – students are sent on errands to avoid them being seen by important visitors. Senior leaders often support the cover-up of a problem child to protect the school's reputation. Of course, these students could be permanently excluded as a way of solving the matter altogether, but that might affect the performance table data …

Badly behaved students may indeed have a negative impact on groups. Getting rid of the child is the easy option, but is it the right thing to do? Is it the only way?

The 'difficult' child

It was a Thursday afternoon in the learning mentor offices. I was in my second year in education as a project coordinator. My confidence was increasing as my observations continued. However, I had not made the leap into teaching yet. I was typing away at a document, my mind wandering forward to the prawn sandwich I was going to have for lunch. As I glanced out of the window, I spotted a Year 9 boy seated in the waiting area just outside. He was well known as a difficult-to-teach child. 'He's probably been kicked out again,' I thought as I rose to 'deal' with him.

Actually, he was subdued. He sat there silently with a pained expression. 'What's happened now?' I asked, in a not too unfriendly, but also a 'we both know you're in trouble', kind of way. He managed a strained smile. 'I hurt myself this morning,' he grunted through gritted teeth. I was not a first-aider so I called one of the other mentors out to have a look. When he lifted his trouser leg, we both nearly fainted in horror at the bone sticking out of his skin. He'd snapped his leg in PE during lesson one. I don't mean this as an exaggeration: he had snapped his leg!

Period one was hours ago and he had walked around the school gritting his teeth ever since. He didn't complain. He didn't scream. He sucked it up and soldiered on. The nearest he came to emotion was when the ambulance turned up and gave him a mask filled with something to ease the pain. A single tear fell from his eye in what I am assuming was relief. Once he had left, there would not have been enough coffee cups in the staffroom to hold the tears that fell from my eyes when reflecting on this horrific incident.

Where does it come from – this soldiering on, no matter how much pain you are in? I later learned that it is common for neglected children not to cry.[1] They have learned from an early age that crying or complaining doesn't get them the attention they

> How much do you know about the lives of your most difficult learners? Is there ever an excuse to give up on them?

need. So we were witness to an extreme example of neglect. In class, he was loud, annoying and difficult. At home, he was probably unloved and got little attention.

Many years after this experience, I would think back to that wounded child and it would remind me that the 'difficult' child needs to be understood.

---

1   For more on this see Cynthia Crosson-Tower, *Understanding Child Abuse and Neglect*, 9th edn (Upper Saddle River, NJ: Pearson, 2013).

Observation

There's always one child who drives you mad, even if you have given yourself the top sets and tried to keep your classes perfect. Perhaps she won't follow instructions. Perhaps he shouts out at any given opportunity. Perhaps she refuses to come into your lesson because she hates your subject.

Look through the eyes of these children. What are they screaming out for through their poor behaviour? I'm not suggesting that we should give up on behaviour management and teaching in favour of a cuddle club. Not at all. Discipline is necessary, but it must come arm in arm with love and understanding.

How can you work with your most difficult children, and not just banish them from your lessons? You can't be held responsible for the energies that your 'problem' child might bring into your classroom, but you are responsible for the energy that you bring. Make a conscious choice about those energies and make them count.

Do you put your energy into punishment
without examining the issue? Why?

Do you expend your energy in feeling terrible about
particular situations? How does that go?

Do you put all of your energy into the other children who are
behaving well? How does this affect the problem?

Do you put energy into complaining about the child?
Does this help the situation to change?

One particularly unruly Year 7 class I taught had a leader: an 11-year-old girl with the loudest mouth ever to grace a classroom. You knew she had arrived and you knew she was there. Her loud protests about anything they were asked to do made it almost impossible to teach the other children. Her energy was infectious and the rest of the class would giggle and shout alongside her, stopping any meaningful learning in its tracks.

It is tough being a teacher in this situation, so I could not help reacting to her energy too. I needed to step back and observe without letting my emotions take over. She got annoyed at me for doing this during one lesson. She shouted even louder and interrogated me as to why I would not shout back. The other kids in the class joined in: 'Miss, if you just shout at us we will calm down.' Interesting, did they want to be shouted at? Of course not, they just wanted me to put on a show. They wanted to see if they could make me lose my temper. I would be better off observing the problem carefully and trying out solutions that might evoke a leader of learning in this child, instead of a leader of mayhem.

The solution-focused question I settled on was: *how can I get this child to choose positive learning behaviours?* My initial observation was that she was an attention-seeker. She needed to be seen by everyone in the class and had no respect for teachers or rules. She had been told that she had behavioural problems, although there was no official diagnosis from a professional, and she often used this as an excuse to get out of punishments. Her reading skills were weak and she had little self-confidence when it came to learning – although she was abounding in self-confidence when speaking to the whole

> Who is your problem child? Have you ever observed the problem?

class. She seemed to think that if she could wind me up, and make the class laugh, she would be rewarded with their respect. The rest of the class took her lead; they were calmer when she was not in the room. Her energy was fun (if you weren't the teacher!) but she brought life to the lesson. She was the eldest of six children and was used to being the boss. At home she had learned that she needed to have the loudest voice in the room just to be heard.

Through her eyes, I saw myself as yet another teacher telling her what to do. I meant nothing to her and my feelings did not seem to matter. I didn't exist for her as a human being outside of the school walls. Learning gave her little reward, so it was much more fun to mess around than get on with the tasks. She saw herself as the leader of this group, just as she was the leader at home.

Solution

I needed to use her energy to infect everyone positively. If I could get her to give off a calming vibe, and feel satisfaction from behaving in this new way, might this influence her behaviour in subsequent lessons? I went to meet with her during registration time. She was expecting a telling off, which is what she had experienced many times before. She did not get it.

'I've been so impressed with your energy,' I said at the outset. 'It was a little loud last lesson but your energy was so infectious that the rest of the class caught it too. Did you notice that?' Her cynicism against teachers wasn't dissipated by my opening gambit, but I could sense some intrigue in her not overly negative response. I added, 'You remind me of my own children.' This was not entirely untrue. My youngest enjoys winding his sister up and has told me before that he is not sure that she is even human! The eyebrow raise that followed this statement told me that she had just become aware of my humanity. 'I want to try a little experiment next lesson and I can't do it without you. Would you be willing to help?'

Testing the solution

In the next lesson, we were going to explore characters' emotions using Roald Dahl's *Matilda*.

Prior to the lesson we had discussed how she could embody any emotion and support the class in feeling it too. She could use her 'superpower' to help me get the class to understand what it was like to be Matilda. Notice that I had transformed her 'problem' into a superpower for learning. She'd had many years of feeling that education was not something she was very good at, so my goal was to get her to feel satisfaction from learning. My starting point was to get her to take part positively in classroom activities.

We played around with voices for different parts. She stood next to me in a supporting role as I delivered sections of the text to her peers. 'How was Matilda feeling?' she would ask them after portraying Matilda's thoughts in role. The class responded, and she took down their responses on our whiteboard. In the previous lesson, she would have shouted me down and made every attempt to destroy my efforts. In this lesson, she was prepared to participate.

Review

This was not the most testing of lessons to set up. We had a chat, made agreements, decided on roles and then I let her take a leading role in the delivery. She sat close to me and took my lead, now feeding off my calm rather that fuelling others with her crazy. She was an amazing help.

Finding a strategic role in each lesson for my 'problem' child was not difficult, and she slowly learned how to give others a voice. Calm ensued and we had a wonderful few months together as a class. Now willing to learn, I was able to properly assess her learning needs and create desirable difficulties that helped her to feel the satisfaction that learning can bring. Without the intervention, we may have simply struggled on.

Try this!

It can be difficult to keep your cool when a problem arises in the middle of a lesson. Having a reflective tool to hand can be a useful physical reminder that you are at the start of a problem-solving cycle.

If a child is causing problems in your classroom, have a go at filling in the chart below. A problem only remains a problem if you do nothing about it. Take the energy that you might spend correcting them, shouting at them and getting irritated by them, and instead plough it into a purposeful step forward. This tool should not take up much of your working day. However, you will need to find time to investigate, talk to others and get a clearer picture than the one you see in your classroom. You can fill in parts discreetly during the lesson, but ensure the student is not aware that you are observing them. This would single them out and bring more attention to them.

Try not to see this as more pointless paperwork; rather, as the stepping stone to a resolution. Test out the solutions you create one by one. Don't attempt to try too many things at once, as you won't get a proper understanding of what works and what doesn't. Observe the impact of your interventions and return to the problem chart with your results. If the intervention worked, make a note of your success and file away this important information. You may have a similar situation in future and will want to use past successes to inform your next steps. If your intervention doesn't work immediately, don't give up! People are complicated. The more effort you put into getting to know your students, the more likely it is that you will solve the problems and remove any barriers to learning. Relationships take time.

Remember, working alone will get results but working in a team is better. If you can get a group of teachers together (especially if you are in a secondary setting), all willing to tackle this problem, the power of collaboration may get you to an effective solution faster and with more powerful results.

The example that follows shows how I used this tool for the previous problem. You can find a blank copy of the Self-Observation Tool in the Resource Cupboard.

	Notes	Learning barriers caused	Questions arising
Entering the class	Always last to turn up. Unsettles other students with interactions as she enters.	Whole-class disruption. The start of the lesson is slowed down.	How can I get her to want to be on time?
Individual tasks	Rarely completes work. Takes this time to unsettle others. Great at talking. Loses attention when doing.	Other students distracted, leading to incomplete work.	How can I get her to feel a sense of reward from completing work?
Group work	Loudest in the group. Often needs to be separated to work alone after disruptive behaviour. Likes to work with J but has a negative influence on J's work rate.	Demonstrates no ability to work in a team. Difficult to set collaborative tasks.	How can I use her power to become a leader in the group rather than a disruptor?
Peer interaction	Friends with M and K outside of class. Has a difficult relationship with K. Rude to classmates. Rude to students who try to remain on task. Not afraid to talk in front of peers.	Students don't want to be seen as working. They are afraid of peer judgement.	How can this power be used to make her a leader of learning?

	Notes	Learning barriers caused	Questions arising
Adult interaction	No fear of consequences. Rude to most staff members. Doesn't follow rules. Has a great relationship with pastoral staff; however, uses this relationship negatively. She once left the room to bring head of year along to tell me that she can move seats when she wants to.	Uses 'behaviour problem' as an excuse to avoid learning.	Can we turn a behaviour problem into a superpower for learning? Could this be a unique skill, not a hindrance?
Information from other adults	Has shown an interest in acting as a career. 'Behaviour problem' is unconfirmed and has not been diagnosed. Similar behaviour across the curriculum. Low reading age.	Low reading age may make learning feel difficult.	Is her reading age the reason behind avoiding tasks? How can we turn the interest in acting into something that makes learning accessible?

	Notes	Learning barriers caused	Questions arising
Home understanding	Eldest of six children.	Perhaps attention-seeking comes from attempts to get attention at home?	Being the eldest, is she used to being in charge? Could we put her in charge of something that helps bring a more positive energy into the room?
Actions based on observations:			
Plan an accessible lesson that puts N in charge. Take reading level into account and prepare with the text beforehand.			
Use interest in acting as part of the lesson and turn the 'problem' into a superpower.			
Meet with N to discuss these plans and provide preparation work for her role.			

We are responsible for the energy we put into solving or ignoring a problem. Think about the wasted resources if we don't attempt to solve things through creativity, questioning, observation and trying out different methods. All of these things take up our time, but they can also save the pointless dissipation of energy through shouting and frustration. The energy spent on tackling this problem led to powerful learning and a change in attitude from a child who otherwise might have grown older never knowing that learning could be so rewarding. No matter what the 'problem' is, there is always a solution if you stop, look and try.

Chapter 4

NO NEED TO WORRY ABOUT THEM – THEY'RE CLEVER!

Challenging our students is about much more than asking harder questions. Students of all levels can experience the joy that comes from education and learning. If, as teachers, we only have eyes for the exam they need to pass, how many of our students will never feel that joy?

Mrs P was a well-established teacher. She took all of the top sets and had the formula for A* nailed. There was no messing about with group work in her lessons. No thinking for themselves. Why would they need to think when they had her? Memorise the formula and you were guaranteed to pass. All you had to be was a bright listener who was great at taking notes and your future was mapped out. 10X1 belonged to Mrs P. They had belonged to her since Year 8 and were well versed in her ways: sit down, get your pen out and prepare to have all you need poured into your brain. She loved them and knew that her methods would get them the grade they deserved. They loved her in return and knew that listening would get them the grade they needed.

July was approaching and the news spread fast among the students: Mrs P was retiring … What would Year 11 bring?

Spoon-feeding

Mrs P is not alone. Many Mrs Ps still exist. They have the exam specification down to a T and are filled with considerable wisdom. They are invaluable to schools. From Mrs P's perspective, she is doing the right thing. She has been employed to get the students the best grade possible, and that is exactly what she does. But looking at the bigger picture – over the longer term – what impact does this approach have on the students' future education? How does life go on once she is no longer available to spoon-feed them?

Teachers with top sets could (and do) get away with spoon-feeding. As a novice classroom assistant observing this way of teaching from the cupboard, I remember thinking that it was amazing. Even 9Z3 would sit down, shut up and listen in Mrs P's classroom. However, when looked at from the perspective of the students in the classroom, and the teacher who takes over when Mrs P retires, this way of teaching begins to lose its gloss.

Taking on a high-achieving class from a well-established teacher who churns out top grades year after year can be tough for teachers who expect independence from their students. It is also tough for the students when they discover that their new teacher is unwilling to spoon-feed them for the exam. Teachers who want independent learners often experience a backlash: 'Just tell us the answer!' Of course, the students don't want to fail, but often they don't want to have to think for themselves either.

In my experience, it is typically the well-behaved elite who are spoon-fed from an early age. They will sit quietly taking reams of notes as their teacher reads from the syllabus. Do it in this way. Answer it like that. Add this sentence for an extra point. As well as this approach being spirit-crushingly boring, these students are not being stretched (other than to the edge of boredom). They are like trained monkeys, excellent at following instructions, but do they know why they're doing what they're doing?

Not all students in high-attaining classes remain switched on. Have you experienced the bright yet bored learner? The child in the top set who should be getting an A* but chooses to avoid working and makes your life a misery? 'You've got so much potential,' you scream as they lazily ignore you and churn out another dog-and-homework excuse. Many capable children are turned off by the exam factory they are forced to endure. We need to give them a better purpose than just passing exams. There has to be more to justify fourteen years in education than taking an exam at the end, right?

Wasted

Try to look at the situation from the perspective of a bright but bored child:

> Starting off on the right road to school, I go straight past our supplier's house and don't usually make it all the way any more. He always has a good stash of vodka and cigs to sell at the right price for a kid at school. The river is free from prying eyes most of the day, so we settle down to another day of drinking.
>
> It's been a week since I walked the whole way there. School has been boring the shit out of me for ages. At nearly 16, it's bored me enough to snatch as many sunny days by the river as I can. They'd contact home soon but I would deal with that when the day came. Freedom's always worth it. Anyway, the punishment for skipping school is getting suspended – win-win!
>
> How many hours have I already wasted in a maths classroom? It could be fun but there are only so many times you can get sent out for winding the teacher up to the point of hysterics before that gets boring too. I love doing drama but there weren't enough places on the course to let me keep doing it beyond Year 9. They didn't want a kid like me messing it up for them anyway. Kicked out of science and PE for bad behaviour. Removed from the business course for lack of effort. Nobody ever tells me why I'm there. It's a prison to keep us from being

free until we're old enough to work. There's only English worth turning up for, and even then they don't let me write stories.

They try to talk to me sometimes. 'You're a clever girl but you're wasting it,' Mr S tried to tell me one day. He's nice but he's old. He hasn't got a clue. They don't understand. There's only another year to go until I'm free of them and their 'concern'. The mates I'm with know how I feel. They show me how to find the freedom I'm craving much earlier than school will let me taste it. It tastes like vodka mixed with lager. It tastes like the shackles have been lifted and a world of slightly fuzzy edges and fun emerges in its place. It tastes good, and I keep tasting it to make the monotony go away.

Max has got a clue. He's finished school now but he can still remember how it felt. 'They're wasting your time! Exams count for nothing, so don't listen to them.' If he hasn't got a job yet after being in education from age 4, neither will I. He knows what he is talking about. He is me, only older. Why go to school when it's all pointless information I'll never use again? I'll down another drink instead.

Give me a reason to put down this bottle and I'll get back in my seat. Why am I learning this? To get a job? To pass exams? To prepare for life? Life can prepare me for life. School would just prepare me to be bored, if I'd let it. I don't know what I want to be. I just know I don't want to be bored.

My friend fell in the river. It took a while to drag her out but she lived. Good job we brought our own clothes. Imagine explaining to your parents how your uniform got that wet. 2.30pm and it's time to go. My head is fuzzy from the sun and shots, but it's been a day well spent. Nobody will be home when I get back. I can sleep it off. 'Same again tomorrow,' we say and leave, back down the same path we came.

Bright and bored. That was me. The above is a small part of the autobiography I will never write. It is also a true story for many children lost in our school system today. There seems to be so much more out there than learning when you are young and have no idea what education is about. I was under the radar as a learner, but I put myself above the radar as a troublemaker. As a result of my poor behaviour and apathy, I was mostly in middle sets at school. There were plenty of allies to help me avoid learning and plenty of teachers willing to remove me from the classroom.

Many of my teachers taught in this spoon-feeding way, no matter what set I found myself in. 'Can you begin by saying …' We would smirk at each other in our English class – the teacher always started his dictation like this and never asked for our point of view. Lessons were by rote and we were expected to sit down, shut up and listen.

I had been placed in top sets for certain subjects and those classes were very different – in that nobody wanted to play with me. The teachers took us strictly through the syllabus and I sat there bored but behaving. Where was the challenge? Where was the development of skill? What the hell was the purpose beyond the exam? 'What's the point in this?' I would regularly ask, and get the generic reply, 'It's for your exam.' From the teachers' perspective, I probably seemed like a cheeky child who was interrupting and questioning for the sake of

> How many of your high-attaining students' names do you know?

it. In reality, I really wanted to find out why. I really wanted to know why I was putting myself through this when there was so much more to life that could be enjoyed.

Their uninspiring answers led me to skipping school, refusing to do homework and enjoying daily detentions (that I never turned up for). How different it might have been if I had discovered that I was way more than middle of the road and capable of great things. All I needed was a purpose, but nobody seemed to care. I passed most of my exams (even in the subjects I'd been removed from for my poor behaviour), but I didn't really understand what or why I was learning. Information was dictated for me to memorise. I preferred to hang out by the river.

These formative experiences were early versions of the cupboard (although I had no idea at the time). My memories of school help to give me perspective when my students ask, 'What's the point in this, Miss?' My answer is never, 'The exam' (although I make sure they are ready to pass these too). I make sure the learning has real purpose before I begin to teach.

It wasn't until the age of 21 – sitting in a cupboard and peering through the gap in the door – that I experienced how amazing learning can be. I realised that my teachers could have brought that joy to me so much earlier, if they had known how and why. Now I thrive on learning new things. Forgive the cliché, but I am an official member of the lifelong learner club and I want to get my students to sign up too.

Do you actively seek to challenge students
with high prior attainment? How?

Do you teach to the test without teaching them the why? Why?

Do you think about the next step for your
students after they leave you?

Do you consider how your students would
survive if you were suddenly gone?

Do you think from the perspective of your students?

Observation

Taking over from a well-established spoon-feeder, it took some time to get the new 11X1 on side. They wanted their old teacher back and thought that I was hard work. I could see their point of view: they were afraid of change and feared that this new way of working might result in failure. From my point of view, I knew that beyond the exams they were about to take, their reliance on a teacher would hold them back in work or higher education.

If we make learning choices based on trends in education or our own personal way of working, we are looking only at ourselves and not at the bigger picture. To be able to support students on their journey to independence, I needed to observe their learning behaviours carefully in order to employ the right methods that would take them from being passive to active learners.

11X1 were great at answering the questions I set for them. However, I wanted to know how well they could choose their own questions at a level appropriate to their current understanding. Did they understand that gathering knowledge was as important as higher order thinking? The class had high prior attainment and lots of knowledge. This meant that when setting them tiered starter tasks (i.e. easy, moderate and difficult questions), they would immediately go for the highest level. My observations told me

> Do you value students being able to think for themselves?

that they valued intelligence over effort. They believed that they were naturally capable and so should always go for the hardest task or they would be lesser students.

A student with low prior attainment has to try harder for success. Hopefully they learn that accomplishment comes through effort, so without effort they will fail. For many high-attaining students, all they need is to be told how to pass the exam and they do it. Very little effort is required – the teacher has done the work and they regurgitate it verbatim. Following success in their GCSEs and A levels, these students move seamlessly on to higher education. However, many high-achieving young people crumble at this point because they don't understand why they suddenly have to put effort into subjects that came easily to them before. 11X1 clearly had this mindset.

Solution

My question for investigation was: *how could I get them to feel the importance of effort in learning?* To stretch the more able, I wanted to hone their effort habits, making these an important part of the learning process. The problem was that my class were always getting the answers right. They weren't feeling the struggle that comes from taxing learning. I could have had an easy life and avoided the effort of teaching them this; however, it would only hit harder when they reached higher education.

Testing the solution

My goal was to teach the students the importance of knowledge, so I set them a tiered task in which the higher levels would test them to their limits. The task was not impossible, but it was only possible with effort – only they did not know that yet.

I used the Structure of Observed Learning Outcome (SOLO) taxonomy (a beginner's guide can be found in the Resource Cupboard), a model developed by John Biggs and Kevin Collis, to set the levels.[1] Each task had to be covered before the next one could take place.

1. Unistructural: exploring plot and character.

2. Multistructural: finding out about context, meaning, language, interpretations and structure.

3. Relational: writing an account based on their knowledge.

4. Extended abstract: a task that required them to link their multistructural knowledge and use that relational understanding to think for themselves.

---

1   For more on this see John B. Biggs and Kevin F. Collis, *Evaluating the Quality of Learning: The SOLO Taxonomy* (New York: Academic Press, 1982).

Note that I always start my questioning at unistructural as this is the first step on the ladder of understanding. Prestructural is the stage before any learning has taken place (or perhaps if the students have a misconception about something they have learned).

The tasks were based on a novel we had not covered before, which meant that most, if not all, students would have to start from scratch. I asked them to enter the room in silence and choose their task based on the learning outcome.

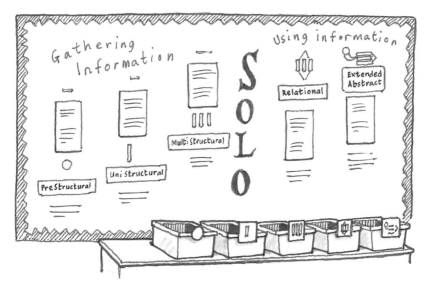

The students chose their own tasks from the SOLO buckets. Each student began by choosing the task with the highest level of difficulty.

The outcome was clearly displayed: to explore and respond to *Wuthering Heights*. We had not read the novel. We had not so much as looked at the front cover. A student with a realistic insight into their level of learning would have looked at the outcome, realised that they were starting from zero and begun their thinking from the very first box. Predictably, this class didn't. They went to the extended abstract without question.

I observed their struggle as they sat silently in their seats. They immediately began to realise that they couldn't answer the question – they simply did not have the relevant knowledge. They grimaced and scratched their heads and looked around nervously. Slowly, one by one, they began to return to the SOLO boxes. They replaced their extended abstract question with the unistructural task and found that they could now engage.

I stopped the class to dissect what had just happened. We explored why they had gone directly to the most difficult box and how they felt when they couldn't answer the question. Ultimately, a light bulb had been turned on with respect to the importance of knowledge. Not knowing something doesn't mean you are stupid. It simply means you haven't learned it *yet*. Nor does knowing something make you inherently intelligent. There is a learning process for every subject, and that means no shortcuts – we can't jump over the steps of the learning process. But the more we know, the easier it is to relate our knowledge to tasks.

> How do you create challenge for high attainers? Does it ever go beyond the exam?

Review

Directly experiencing the importance of knowledge gave the students an understanding of the process of learning. They now understood the importance of facts as a foundation for the next steps. They understood why finding out information – beyond what we had time to examine in the classroom – could support them in more difficult analysis down the line. Although none of this was necessary for passing their first set of exams, it was necessary to set them up for lifelong learning. Their safe 'failure' highlighted that

> Have you ever been lazy with a class just because they are well behaved? What effect might this have on their future?

failure can happen to anyone if they aren't active in their own learning. It was a lesson well spent!

Stretching and challenging high attainers doesn't always mean harder questions. Sometimes it can mean recognising the importance of basic knowledge in the bigger picture or of understanding the learning process itself. This is a challenge for most adults as well as children.

Challenge your students to appreciate the processes involved in learning new concepts. Some students may believe that they are 'stupid' and will never learn anything, while higher sets may assume that they are 'talented' and that learning comes easy to them. Both of these self-concepts ignore the learning journey.[2]

Have you stopped to look from all perspectives in this classroom?

Have you explored the students' journey from behind their eyes, or just thanked god that this particular journey feels easy for you as they do everything you say?

Is there one child you know who could achieve but who is switched off?

Do you avoid doing anything about it because the collective value-added that will come from the other bright students will mask this child's failure in your appraisal?

What problems could you solve if you were to step into the cupboard and look carefully at this class? Where are they? Where are they going?

How can you support them to be better learners, even though they are seemingly A-grade students?

---

2   What we are talking about here is growth and fixed mindsets. For detailed information on this topic, it is worth reading Carol Dweck's *Mindset: The New Psychology of Success* (New York: Random House, 2006).

Try this!

A teacher who is alert to the view from the cupboard will know that problems in high-attaining classes are often masked by good behaviour. Their learning behaviours might seem perfect – they may listen attentively and write down every word you say. You could sit back and relax for the year – but is that a creative problem-solving attitude? The problem here may not be immediately apparent, but there is more to learning than passing exams. Keep their futures in mind as you use the Worst/Best Ladder to Success to dissect their present.

First, use the figure on the left to note down everything you possibly can about the worst behaviours of passive high-attaining students. Then use the figure on the right to note down the opposite of those problems or the best-case scenario. What would they be behaving like in a perfect world?

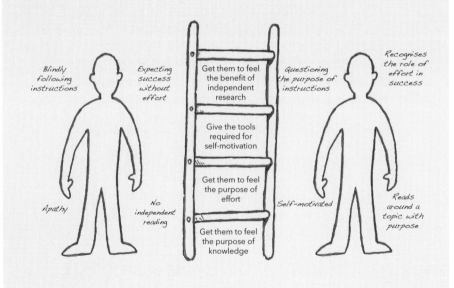

Next, use the ladder in the centre to begin to think of ways in which you are already tackling these behaviours, as well as noting down solution-focused questions to investigate what you might do differently to improve the learning behaviours. Basically, what steps are you taking to transform the worst into the best? What steps do you need to take to solve this problem? Remember: a problem stays a problem if you don't take action to solve it. This task may seem simple but this reflection time can be very powerful. A blank copy of this resource is available in the Resource Cupboard at the end of the book.

Challenging students who believe they are talented can be tricky. If these students fail at something, they can quickly switch off as it is not something they are used to experiencing. The unfamiliar discomfort of failure can lead them to avoid trying. They may have passed their first set of exams by being spoon-fed, but what happens at the next level? What happens during their degree? If students are to be lifelong learners, they need to know how learning works, how to learn for themselves and how to be fully engaged in the process.

Chapter 5

THEY'LL NEVER MAKE IT THROUGH!

Is there such a thing as empathy or is it just sympathy disguised? Your home life may have 2.4 children, reading books at bedtime and a strict 'please and thank you' routine, but what is the home life of your students like? Harrowing stories that could make your nose bleed from crying? Can you make a difference to these children?

Emotional intelligence doesn't mean giving in to demands and letting students off if they swear in your face because their young life is tough. As teachers, how can we teach children to take control of their future, no matter how stormy their present? How can we avoid them becoming trapped in a cycle of low aspiration? We need to understand the power of negative cultures and know our roles in changing them. Teachers often admit defeat with children from poor or violent backgrounds, so does this mean they are abandoned for life?

Observation

On supply in a school in the North East, I overheard a conversation about the new cohort coming up from primary school. It was noted that a child from a notorious family was among the new recruits. The senior leader who had instigated the conversation was having a great laugh about how children from this family never made it past Year 8, so this child would be no different.

The discussion continued about the many other children from this family and their various misdeeds over the years.

My heart sank. This child had no hope. He was already scarred by his name. He had a deprived background and his role models had all been kicked out of mainstream schooling at an early age. What hope did he have if the teachers who were employed to educate him had already decided that his fate was sealed?

Every child should be given a fair chance. Teachers and leaders are in a position of power. They control what happens in their classrooms and schools. If the school has a culture of judgement, what hope do the students have? Power can be, and is, misused by many. How do you ensure that your power is channelled for the good of every child?

Philip Zimbardo conducted his famous Stanford Prison Experiment in 1971. His aim was to observe the effects of perceived power using randomly selected students who became 'prisoners' and 'prison officers'. The simulation was made to feel real and, within days, the experiment had to be shut down because of its negative impact on the participants. Even Zimbardo admitted that he had been absorbed by his role as the governor. He allowed things to happen that were morally wrong and even became paranoid that a released prisoner was returning to free the rest of the inmates. Even though the participants knew they were all playing a role, the roles began to play them. Prison culture took over these 'ordinary' young men. It brought out sadistic behaviour in the guards and riotous behaviour in the prisoners.[1] Don't underestimate the power of culture.

> Have you ever judged a child before you met them?

What culture does your school/classroom have? Are the teachers the guards and the students the prisoners? After hundreds of years of prison culture, crime remains a constant in society. If prison really worked, would crime still

---

1   Zimbardo's book, *The Lucifer Effect: How Good People Turn Evil* (New York: Random House, 2007) was informed by the experiment.

exist? If you are in role as a guard – the authoritarian who holds power over your helpless inmates – how long before your charges revolt? They may be polite to your face but what happens behind your back? Are they learning to live and learn, or to behave and follow instruction? What purpose does this have for them in the future? Are certain inmates labelled as having no hope of ever being educated enough to escape a life of poverty or crime? Are some already failures before they have even had a chance to find out their potential? If this was you, how would you react to knowing that you didn't have what it takes to succeed? Would it infuriate you if you had to attend school every day without any reward at the end of your sentence? Would you turn on the guards who kept you incarcerated? Would you try to make sure you got out of there as soon as possible to stop the torture of zero hope?

One school I worked in allowed the children's disadvantaged home culture to permeate the school walls. A strong learning culture had not been created within the school, which felt more like a prison. 'Our students don't behave well – it's just the way they are,' a classroom assistant told me. 'They are not taught manners at home so we can't get them to be good here.' If this was the view of the staff, then I could see why they had behaviour problems with their students. Could I create a culture of learning in such an environment? Could I create powerful lessons that had purpose beyond the classroom when such a negative culture existed? Or would I find that the classroom assistant was right? That, despite my best efforts, nothing could be done for children who came from underprivileged backgrounds? I was determined to find out.

Solution

My class was a Year 11 group. A group, therefore, who had been at the school for almost five years, who had experienced the culture both without and within, and who, I was told, I had no chance of helping. They were a 'bottom set' and I was warned about their poor behaviour. The advice was: don't have the boys and girls in the same room as they will fight with each other; put one group in the computer room with the classroom assistant. They were not expected to achieve anything so I could do whatever I wanted with them. Horrified that the students were being seen for what they were, not what they could become, I was determined to avoid this advice. They would become my experiment.

After gathering as much data as I could on the class, I created the solution-focused question: *how can I create a culture of learning for a group that are seen by many as a lost cause?* Thinking through the learning skills that I could instil, I focused my attention on effective communication. If I could get them to communicate with me, and with each other, our lessons would have purpose. Even if they didn't have time to learn enough to pass the exam, good communication skills would help them in their future learning, in interviews and in life.

We were approaching the end of their final year at school, so all I had with the class was six weeks. Nonetheless, I planned to repeat the same lesson at least three times with the intention of creating confidence by the end of our six weeks together. My plan was to stick with the same skill and rehearse it over and over before allowing them to put the skill into practice for themselves. I wanted to build their confidence in communicating properly, not fill their heads with one-off ideas. Three lessons would be dedicated to a divergent discussion in which we would explore engaging issues, learn to take turns, articulate responses and build a clear argument. They would then use these skills to create their own presentation on a topic of their choice.

Testing the solution

A divergent question allows students to take a variety of routes. This choice was part of the hook for learning. If I had asked them a closed question – such as, 'Do you like turnips?' – the debate would have been over very quickly. Similarly, if I had asked them, 'What is your favourite TV programme?' there may have been some variation in response but the debate would not have been as fruitful. I gave them a choice of three people to save – Robert, Marni or Roberta. As they entered, I told them that these three people remained on-board a sinking ship. Two would go down with the ship and only one could have a place in the lifeboat. This got their attention.

Initially, I let them make a snap decision and give their responses. As expected, students' replies were one-word answers.

Me: Who did you pick?

Student: Marni.

Me: Why?

Student: Coz she's fit.

Well, it was a start ... Next, I asked them to turn to their partner and try to come up with as many reasons to save their favourite as they could. This exercise aimed to teach them the skill of taking turns. Person 1 had thirty seconds to talk. Person 2 had a much harder job – they had to listen. This is not as easy as it sounds!

Try this!

Sit with your partner or a friend and ask them to tell you something about their day. What they talk about is not important, but it does need to be something engaging about which they can speak at length. As they talk, notice that your mind pings to things you want to say in response: 'Oh, I did that too ...' 'I remember when the same thing happened to me ...' and so on. You are not fully listening to them – you are thinking about you. Don't worry, this is normal. Every time your mind pings to your own response, let it go. Empty your mind, be present and listen. Don't stare at them intently without moving (that's just weird). You can use back channelling such as nodding, agreeing or making sounds to show you

> Do you ever really listen?

are listening, but you can't jump in until it is your turn. This is what I taught the students in the paired part of the lesson.

Next, the students joined with another pair to make a group of four. By escalating from an individual response to a pair and finally to a group, I found that those students who usually sit back have already spoken up and been listened to – their point has been validated by another person – so they are more confident about speaking up within the group. I also found that those students who naturally take over may still do so, but they tend to state each person's point rather than just giving their own.

Thought bombing

I wanted the students to challenge information that had been given to them – to question and explore – so I introduced thought bombs into the group discussion.

The example for this lesson showed three different people on-board a sinking ship. Who are the students going to save? This could be adapted for characters from novels or poems (in English), exploring the lives and decisions of historical figures (in history), looking at cause and consequence (in PSHE), exploring bodily functions (in biology) and so on. The idea is that the students are given a small amount of information, led through turn taking to the group work, and then the thought bombs are thrown in to blow their minds! I usually find that Marni is top of the list to begin with, as she is young and has her whole life ahead of her – but that's before the first thought bomb is delivered …

Our ship is sinking! Only one of us can survive ... who would you pick?

Robert Devlin
A 58-year-old school teacher with three children of his own. Loves fishing at the weekend.

Marni Spence
A 16-year-old schoolgirl. Her worst subject is citizenship and she excels at ICT.

Roberta Maan
A 35-year-old housewife. She loves diamonds!

The thought bomb is a plastic ball – the kind that you find in children's ball pools. It has a small hole in the bottom in which you can insert your explosive thoughts. I roll up slips of paper with new knowledge about the situation and pop them inside the bomb. For example, inside one thought bomb the paper reads: 'Marni is a convicted killer.' And in another we are told of Roberta's charity work and how she fosters children with disabilities. This new information makes the students go 'Ooooooo' and changes the situation entirely. They have much more to take into account when making their decision. The thought bomb explodes current understanding and forces the students to look at the situation from a different point

> How important is communication in your classroom?
>
> Do you expect students to communicate clearly?
>
> Do you teach them how?

of view. The full list of Thought Bombs for Divergent Questioning can be found in the Resource Cupboard.

Creating an argument

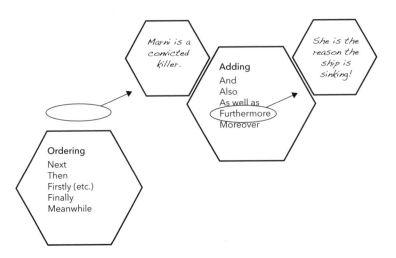

The final step in this lesson is to create an argument to save the person the group has chosen. The students use hexagons to note down individual ideas about why they should or should not save each character. The hexagons can then be joined together to create a speech. The hexagons are like flash cards (in later lessons, the students progress to creating flash cards for their talks). Conjunctive adverbs are pre-printed on another set of hexagons to help the students structure their speeches before presenting them (a set of these are available in the Resource Cupboard).

Lesson two followed the same five-step process (i.e. divergent question, turn-taking discussion, group work and thought bombing, development of speech and presentation of speech). By changing the content, but not the process, the class were able to practise the skill of communication in a familiar context.

The nature of the question is not important. It could have been a discussion about characters from a play they had studied (Which one would you invite to tea?). It could have been an argument about lifestyle choices (vegan, meat-eater or fruitarian … you decide). The key point is that it should enable the students to explore ideas for themselves, and there needs to be good potential to create interesting thought bombs to show them there is always more to discover.

The thought bombs were again used during a discussion about society.

In each lesson, I changed the focus so that our discussions stayed fresh, but the skills we were practising, and tools we were using, remained constant. The more varied the content, the better – because the students will be gaining knowledge as well as practising a skill.

If you are going to try this out, you could use questions such as:

- Which country would you choose to live in? (geography)

- Which painting would you hang on your wall? (art)

- Which mathematician has helped us most? (history or maths)

- Which Greek God would you choose to worship? (Classics or project work)

- Should we be vegetarian, vegan or something else? (science)

- Which artist's work would you choose to save? (art)

By the end of the third lesson, the students were ready for their own investigations, and so I asked them to create their own divergent questions. Their outside culture now came into play as they wanted to discuss horses, hunting and motorbikes. They came up with questions such as, 'Which is bike is better?' They used the five-step method in lessons four and five to discuss their questions with their peers and create individual flash cards to prepare their speeches.

By lesson six, the students had begun practising a skill for life with decent execution. They had picked up knowledge about J. B. Priestley's *An Inspector Calls* in one lesson and reviewed three key figures from history in another. Not bad for a group who were not expected to achieve anything.

By repeating this process, I wanted my students to learn to listen to each other's ideas. I wanted them to feel secure in using conjunctive adverbs as part of their speech, and later to transfer this to their writing. I wanted them to feel self-assured when speaking in front of others with the view to them being confident in their speaking and listening assessments.

> What outcome do you want for your students?
>
> What tools or skills do you want your students to be able to use without thinking?
>
> How can you allow them to practise, practise, practise until it becomes natural to them?

Review

Looking through the eyes of these students, I saw that education seemed to have little purpose in their lives. They were written off by most teachers and controlled rather than taught. My question – *how can I create a culture of learning for a group that are seen by many as a lost cause?* – was answered quite simply. Find something purposeful to teach them. Repeat, repeat and repeat in a varied way to hold their attention and keep them practising. I did not see any of them as a lost cause. Who am I to judge another person's life? I am a teacher and as such it is my job to find a way to teach that will have maximum impact, no matter what their starting point is or how little time I have with them.

Racist!

In another school, 100% white British, in a small town, away from which people very rarely moved, I used the same technique to change the students' thinking. Barring the local takeaways and corner shops (for which the kids still used very derogatory names, presumably picked up from their parents), there was very little cultural diversity. Unfortunately, the students had a tendency to be racist. I could have told them that they were being discriminatory and sanction them for it – in other words, the prison guard approach. It might have stopped the behaviour in the classroom, but it was unlikely to have a long-term impact as these views were common among their peer group. Instead, I tried a little thought bombing on them.

> Do you ignore the problems your community face, thinking you can do nothing about their negative cultures?

The lesson was the same as described with the Year 11 class but with a few tweaks: Robert became Faisal, a Pakistani man; Roberta became a Kuwaiti called Aaliyah; Marni remained white British but her origins and future had been changed – she had emigrated to China from Sunderland. The thought bombs contained information about each person's family's movements across the generations, with the aim of getting the students to question their narrow thinking. I wanted them to interrogate their own racism, not tell them to stop thinking that way! This had a powerful impact on their behaviour, which I hope they took back into their community.

How else could you use divergent questions as a tool to get students thinking through their negative attitudes without being chastised into changing them? What issues does your community face that might be explored through thought bombing, questioning and exploration? How can you avoid becoming the judgemental guard and instead work together for a successful change of attitudes and cultures?

Your role in changing negative culture

As a teacher or leader, you are responsible for creating the culture in your classroom and school. You need to get to know the community in which your learners live. What are the positive aspects of their culture? What are the damaging aspects that you could play a part in shifting? Remember, just telling them to change will make very little difference. Helping them to explore different cultures positively using communication, learning tools, questioning, group work and so on is a collaborative way of reaching your goal.

If your school's local area has a negative culture that is following the children into school, you need to find a way of getting them to question their own thinking. How could you create an alternative culture so powerful that it begins to permeate the community? Schools that give in to negative stereotypes ('That's just how our kids are. If you see their parents, you will understand why they are the way they are.') are doing nothing to support positive transformation. By seeing things from the viewpoint of the children, what can you do differently?

I once tried to get a group of teachers at a conference to understand how we can change school culture. I brought along an umbrella and asked how many of the delegates were superstitious. Several people raised their hands. I then asked someone who had not raised their hand to put the umbrella up indoors. They stared at me in horror – was I trying to jinx their day? Everyone knows that you shouldn't put an umbrella up indoors! But they had just said they weren't superstitious.

This bothered me for some time. Why are we scared of such a small thing? Did the person who invented the umbrella summon the power of a curse and lay it on all umbrellas for evermore? This seems a bit farfetched. Determined to understand the source of this superstition, I began researching the origins of umbrellas and found that they were invented in China to stop sunburn. It was commonly said that to put an umbrella up indoors was an insult to the sun. Over time, this has evolved into it being unlucky.

My point is that we make stuff up! But this means we also have the power to change things that are wrong. If cultural beliefs are damaging, we can transform them through education. If children come from a long line of failure, let's help them to find ways to succeed. Let's stop accepting seemingly absolute truths and start questioning for change and success.

Part II

THE VIEW FROM THE CUPBOARD: TEACHERS

Chapter 6

DO YOU REALISE HOW HARD I WORK?

> If you completed the jobs you needed to get done an hour early,
> would you just find something else to add to your list?

Mabel and Rosa were new to the school. They were both brilliant teachers and a great addition to the department. But however hard they tried, nobody could ever work harder than them. It was as if it was a competition!

Mabel: I got in at 7am today, and I'm not going to be done with my marking until at least 7pm tonight.

Rosa: Really? Well I got in at 6am and I'm planning on asking the caretaker to keep the school open for an extra hour so that I can create the new wall display I've been promising to get done. I just won't have time otherwise.

The rivalry was infectious and soon others were joining in: 'I've got so much to do *and* I've got two kids. I'll be working until midnight tonight.' Emails were sent at ungodly hours and lunch breaks were littered with to-do lists as long as Mabel's written notes on her Year 7 classes' homework. Complaints and exhaustion filled the school. Teachers have a tough enough job without it being infected by the 'I work harder than you' plague.

Stop it!

Nobody can work as hard as you work because it is you who is doing the working. You are only in competition with yourself. Your failure to have a sensible work–life balance doesn't lie at the door of the school, with policy makers or with leaders – it lies with you.

Of course, some schools make unreasonable demands on teachers. The worst example I have seen was a spreadsheet that needed to be filled in fortnightly which contained over 400 skills that had to be assessed for progress. Now imagine having eight classes, with thirty kids in each, and you can begin to envisage just how long it took to fill in this spreadsheet. Moreover, the software was difficult to use, with columns that did not easily match up to students' names. It was of no use to anyone. The teachers couldn't extract useful information about their classes, the students weren't able to use it to understand

> What have you missed out on because you put work first?

where they were and what they should do to improve and, as far as I know, it was never used to present information to parents. It was a task created purely for show because the leaders of the school had decided that the inspectors would like it. It was an unnecessary requirement, which teachers complained about behind closed doors but completed out of fear.

If unreasonable demands are being made on your time, you can do something about it. Ask around – are you the only person feeling like this? You are the teacher on the ground and you know what is useful to you and your classes.

> Do you dare take control of your time?
>
> What's the worst that could happen?

Don't follow orders blindly and complain about it in private. You don't have to stay in a school that refuses to change pointless policies. You should not be expected to stay up until midnight completing your work. Take positive action to make the system work for you and your students.

Observation

As a learning leader, my work–life balance got out of kilter. I never attempted to solve the issue at the time because I actually enjoyed this work and it felt purposeful. However, my family suffered due to the pressure I was under, and it took a huge shock to jolt me back to reality. My husband had a stroke one night and I still turned up for training the next day, exhausted but on time. School had become my life, and the little distraction of family had become so distant that I allowed this to happen. This was my fault! I was being self-blind again – this time to my ability to regulate my time and myself.

It is easy to be a lone wolf as a teacher. We have so much responsibility on our shoulders, and we can take on more and more until we find ourselves working twelve hours a day, seven days a week. But remember, that is our choice.

Solution

Have you ever uttered the words, 'I don't have time'? Of course you have time! There is a finite amount of time, but we still have it. It is how we use our time that will either lead to exhaustion or to a healthy work–life balance. If we are struggling with an unmanageable workload, then we have an issue with self-regulation.

How can we create more time in such an impossibly busy career? Here we will consider some of the problems that afflict time-poor teachers and the solutions that will save us from that sick note for stress that is looming on the horizon.

Procrastination

Many teachers (me included) proclaim that they are more efficient when they get the job done at the last minute. However, studies suggest that this form of putting things off can be damaging to your well-being, as Dianne M. Tice and Roy F. Baumeister of Case Western Reserve University summarise:

'Two longitudinal studies examined procrastination among students. Procrastinators reported lower stress and less illness than non-procrastinators early in the semester, but they reported higher stress and more illness late in the term, and overall they were sicker. Procrastinators also received lower grades on all assignments.'[1] The researchers conclude that postponement is a 'self-defeating behaviour pattern' over the long term. The stress of knowing that the job has to be done remains a constant until it is completed. Last minute rush jobs never represent our best work, and how do we cope if an unexpected job arrives just as that last minute job absolutely has to be done? We combust!

Procrastination arises from fear – fear of the job itself, fear of making a mess of it, fear of it taking too long, fear that we don't know how to do it – so we put it off. We tell ourselves that our future self will be able to cope with these feelings much better than we can now. We burden our future self with the stress and pretend to our present self that it's no longer a problem. But it hasn't gone away!

Stalling can take many forms – from doing all of the housework before we begin our 'real' work to staring endlessly at Facebook, numbly observing other people seeming to manage their lives without issue. Whatever form your procrastination takes, it comes from a failure to self-regulate, but that means you have the option to take back control.

---

1   Dianne M. Tice and Roy F. Baumeister, Longitudinal Study of Procrastination, Performance, Stress, and Health: The Costs and Benefits of Dawdling, *Psychological Science* 8(6) (1997): 454-458.

Try this!

What are your procrastination hotspots? There are lots of online procrastination tests you can take – perhaps you have done a few already while procrastinating! They usually include a series of questions designed to help you identify your own difficulties. However, identification is not enough to solve the issue. You have to *do something* with the information you get back.

Here's an example I filled in based on my own habits. A blank version is available in the Resource Cupboard. Rank yourself from 1 to 5 (1 – strongly agree, 2 – slightly agree, 3 – neither agree nor disagree, 4 – slightly disagree, 5 – disagree).

Type		1	2	3	4	5
P	You take at least half an hour to write an email.	X				
P	You agonise over a single word in a document for ages.	X				
P	You waste time trying out fonts, background colours, etc. on a PowerPoint for a single lesson.	X				
I	You are due to deliver a presentation to the school leaders. You can't stop thinking about how they will judge you. You put off doing anything.			X		
I	The thought of showing a senior member of staff your work fills you with dread. You avoid the task to prevent them seeing your faults.			X		
I	You wish someone better than you had been asked to do a particular task. You delay working on it to hide from the guilt.				X	

Type		1	2	3	4	5
M	You would rather tidy your whole house than start this task.		X			
M	Every time you think about the task at hand you get bored. You avoid it!					X
M	The sun is out … you succumb to the temptation to shelve the task entirely.		X			
O	Thinking about the task makes you anxious. You avoid it!			X		
O	You can't see how you will get the task done in the time you have. You avoid it!		X			
O	Huge tasks make you stressed, so you get all of the little jobs done and avoid the bigger tasks.			X		
L	You always leave tasks until the last minute.					X
L	You work better when your back is against the wall.					X
L	You always get it done in the end, so you choose having fun over getting it done early.					X

The crosses that appear in columns 1 and 2 indicate my hotspots. Crosses in columns 3 and 4 are less worrying, but I need to keep an eye on this behaviour to ensure that it does not become a hotspot. Crosses in column 5 are not an area of concern. The type of procrastination is indicated by the letters in the left-hand column. You can read more about this below and get ideas to support you in regulating your own behaviours. I ranked strongest in perfectionism, but notice that the grid has crosses all over the place which indicates a degree of procrastination in other areas too. Recognising where your hotspots are is the first step towards gaining more time by overcoming them. Step two is doing something about it!

P: Perfectionist. You need to recognise that your time is being wasted on the small things. You can't make everything perfect, so if you are spending too much time perfecting small things, you are bound to be doing a bad job somewhere else. You can save time by addressing this hotspot.

+ Get the job done before worrying about what it looks like to others.

+ Only ever compare yourself to yourself.

+ Make 'good enough' your mantra when you find yourself agonising over trivial details.

I: Impostor syndrome. You are avoiding working in order to avoid judgement. Recognise that this is happening. You are more likely to be judged poorly if you rush the work at the last minute so this is a self-defeating action. Recognising this is the first step towards reclaiming this time.

+ Understand your strengths and recognise your capabilities through self-reflection.

+ Talk to other people about how you feel. You will find that individuals who seem to be perfect at their roles suffer with self-doubt too.

+ Recognise your insecurity and overcome it with logic about what you can do, have done and are capable of.

M: Motivation (lack thereof). You are unmotivated by the jobs you need to do. This lack of motivation leads to negative emotions surrounding the act of completing the job. How can you motivate yourself to do the mundane?

- Offer yourself a reward for completing the job.

- Find the purpose beneath the humdrum task.

- If you see all your work tasks as mundane, perhaps you need to consider another career that will offer more challenge?

O: Overwhelmed. When a task seems too big to complete, recognise that postponing it will not make the task any smaller. In fact, it will be the same size as it always was but you will have less time to get it done.

- Look for a way to break big jobs down into smaller chunks.

- Pace yourself over time and feel good as you complete jobs section by section.

- Remind yourself of the research that procrastination may bring short-term benefits but that in the long term, you will suffer.

L: Lucky! Stop it! Your luck will run out one day. You were probably the person at school who crammed the night before the test and were lucky enough to pass. You give in to the positive emotions brought on by doing anything else other than getting your work done. Last minute rushing may work out sometimes, but what if unexpected and important tasks land on your desk without notice and you are left with no time to complete your work? Look around you. Are other people picking up the slack while you have fun?

- Stop telling yourself that you work better when you are doing things last minute.

- Make a schedule for completing tasks and stick to it.

- Don't stop having fun!

This is only a snapshot of potential areas of procrastination. You could try out other ways to observe how you use time and make plans to use it more effectively. Whatever method you use, working on your effort habits will help you to make better use of your time, but don't try to change everything all at once. You may just fall back into overwhelmed and do nothing.

It might sound like a huge waste of time to observe your time, but if you take it seriously the outcome can be worth the effort spent. Knowing how you use your time well can help you to make choices to improve your time management.

Try this!

Once a term, keep a time diary for seven days in which you keep a record of what you are doing. This could be minute by minute or hour by hour. When you review your diary, look out for any wasted time, procrastination hotspots, pointless activities, tasks that could be shared, tasks that could be removed and so on. You may notice that your time is spent rushing through various to-do lists without having planned what you will do and when. Your aim is to claw back a realistic amount of time each day and make a plan about how you will use it more productively. Perhaps planning ahead is the best way for you to save yourself time, but everyone is different. Knowing yourself is key.

There is a blank version of the Time Diary in the Resource Cupboard. As with anything, it is what you do with the results that counts. Keeping a diary shouldn't be about adding to your workload. It should streamline your workload by pinpointing areas in which you are wasting time.

Time Diary		
Date *September*	Aim *To save one hour a day*	
Time	Activity	Notes
7:30am–8am	*Dressing/breakfast*	*Snoozed alarm 5x*
8am–8:30am	*Work – reading emails*	*Not much interesting there ...*
8.30am–10am	*Teaching*	
10am–11am	*Free period*	*Chatted to Martha for half an hour*
11am–1pm	*Teaching*	
1pm–1:30pm	*Lunch*	*Ate at the desk marking*

Failure to plan ahead

Are you seriously difficult to live with once a deadline is imminent? I know I am. On the day this book is due to be handed over, I will be hunched over my computer tapping away furiously as my family cower in another room, afraid to make a noise as the beast will look up and snatch their souls. A tad dramatic? Just try living with a writer whose office is the dining room table! Luckily, I recognise this behaviour in myself and take steps to avoid it. How? By planning ahead.

Know what needs to be done, do it and move on. Set realistic time limits and stick to them. Factor in time for family and friends, and don't back out because a last minute job comes in – unless it is absolutely essential. Planning ahead is about self-regulating and using your diary properly. Not just noting down the dates for deadlines but estimating how much time each task will take, realistically, based on previous experience. It's a good idea to give yourself some time to review your work and make any improvements before the deadline. Do this and watch your stress levels decrease dramatically.

Time, assessment and planning

Take Mabel's marking, for example. She chooses to mark until 7pm. Her marking is lengthy and takes many hours to complete. She mutters, 'I don't have time!' but she has used her time unwisely. How much impact has her three-hour session marking thirty Year 7 homeworks had? Have the students responded to her feedback? Have they begun using capital letters and full stops now that she has lovingly filled them all in? In my experience the answer is no.

Feedback only has impact if it is used by the students to understand what they need to do to improve in their learning. Lengthy feedback – for example, detailed comments on a longer piece of work – can have a positive effect, if you give the students time to process and act upon your feedback. This can be time spent discussing the comments in class with the students, who then have another go at producing a better version of the task. Alternatively, it can be set as a homework task, as long as the students are able to process the information without support. Shorter feedback can often do exactly the same job in less time. There are lots of ideas for reducing the time spent marking books out there – here are a few of my favourites.

Whole-class feedback

Use whole-class feedback when the class are making similar mistakes. Read through all of their work but don't write on it; instead, make a note of any errors or misconceptions on a blank sheet. If one child's work stands out as different, keep that book to one side as you may need to make a separate note or offer some one-to-one support.

Create a task that asks all the students to look again at their errors and correct them. This can be on a printed sheet that is handed out as a starter task in the next lesson, or even projected onto the whiteboard. This has exactly the same effect and takes even less time. Any common misconceptions will need to be explored during further teaching time.

You are marking and planning simultaneously. Win-win in half the time!

Marking routines

Marking routines can help you to manage your workload better. Never ask students to do any written work if you are not going to look at it for three weeks – what's the point? Think carefully about what you want students to do in lessons and how you are going to assess what they have done. Don't set work that is too lengthy for you to mark. Plan ahead for longer pieces of work and ensure that they have genuine purpose. Practising skills such as writing or responding to questions can be done in smaller chunks initially. As these tasks are more focused, they are easier to mark and easier for the students to review and correct.

Don't be afraid to have discussion lessons or lessons that produce no written work if a concept can be learned without it. If students are learning, and you are able to assess their learning through questioning, quizzing, debate or in any other way, don't worry that there is no work in their books. You don't need to provide evidence for every single lesson.

Avoid 'tick and flick' (or catch-up marking)

Tick and flick exercises are not about feedback, they are about making the book look like it has been marked. This vanity exercise is a waste of time for everyone. If you have fallen behind on your marking, get back into a regular routine of students reflecting on their work to date and using lesson time to utilise feedback constructively.

Peer and self-assessment

Peer and self-assessment are great ways to reduce your marking pile. However, if this is the only reason you use this type of assessment, stop right now! Students need to know how to assess their own and others' work. They need to be given guidance and allowed to practise under your supervision. I spend a number of weeks developing a culture of critique in the classroom before I unleash students on one another's work. They need to know how to give feedback that is kind, specific and helpful. Ron Berger's *An Ethic of Excellence* is a great place to start if you are looking to develop a culture of critique.[2]

Two additional areas in which we can save time are:

Not wasting time on faff

Don't spend time developing fancy PowerPoints filled with quirky images and clever animations. If you have a dyslexic child in your class, they won't be able to access them anyway. If you need to project anything, keep it simple. A light-coloured background with simple writing will get across information just as easily as one that has been primped to perfection over several hours. Remember, it's the learning that counts, not what a resource looks like.

Avoiding overcommitment

Mabel, Rosa and I would all fall into the trap of overcommitment. 'Yes! Of course, I'll do that for you. Tomorrow? No problem … Another thing? Sure, add it to my list. I'll get that done for you right away!' If you know you are going to struggle to do all of the tasks on your to-do list, why on earth would you say yes to another one?

---

2   See Ron Berger, *An Ethic of Excellence: Building a Culture of Craftsmanship with Students* (Portsmouth, NH: Heinemann, 2003).

Are you scared of the emotional impact that saying no might have? Do you think that saying no will make you look bad or that the person asking won't like you any more? Do you fear negative professional consequences? Would it affect how you see yourself as a professional who can take on anything?

These all seem like pretty good reasons to add another task to your list. But if you take a step back, you will see that you are not taking control of the situation. You are failing to self-regulate. Who is going to suffer over the longer term? You! And possibly your family when you don't see them for the next month.

You need to get yourself some stock phrases that you can call on whenever you are asked to take on something unexpected that is not part of your official role. Try one of these:

- 'Can I get back to you later today? I need to look at my schedule first.'

    This phrase gives you the chance to go back to the person later, after *really* looking at what you can and cannot handle. If you don't have time, you need to say so.

- 'I would love to help, but I have so much on right now that I wouldn't do a great job.'

    This phrase takes away the possibility of you completing the job. You should use it if you know that you are working at capacity and absolutely couldn't handle anything else.

The person asking might be taken aback, but if you are doing your job – and doing it well – that matters more than showing everyone that you can juggle extra tasks. If you say yes to someone, but don't actually have the time to complete the task, you will resent the person and the job. Why cause yourself additional stress? If you want to do it, are motivated to do it and have the time to do it, then of course say yes. Otherwise, never feel bad about saying no to something that is not part of your everyday role. Save that time for your family.

Testing the solution

Whether you are trying out a more streamlined marking process, developing your skill at avoiding saying yes to everything or working on your procrastination hotspots, you should be testing the process as you go. How well is your new method working? How do you feel as a result of this new method? What has changed in your life? Is this new way of working solving the problems that you faced? If you have chosen something that is making life harder, let it go and try something else. Not all solutions work in practice, but avoiding putting a solution in place because you think it won't work before you've tried it isn't helping either. You are testing the solution to create protocols for your working life. It is worth the reflection!

Review

The next time you find yourself saying, 'I don't have time,' stop, step into the cupboard and observe yourself. Do you see a teacher trying to fit into a culture of working harder than everyone around them, one among lots of other tired teachers? Do you see a procrastinator, unable to get started and rushing to the finish at the last minute? Do you see an overcommitter or a slave to a school that doesn't value their time? No matter which it is, use your reflection to remove the blinkers and reclaim your time. If you are going to be the best teacher you can be, you are going to need that quality time to make improvements. We might have busy jobs but we only have one life. Looking back on a lifetime of stress and busyness is not something you should be aiming for – take control!

Chapter 7
SHE'S JUST A SUPPLY

There is a reason why we should never judge. We are not perfect ourselves. Everyone who works with children should be enabled to be the best they can be. Judging them as *just* a classroom assistant, *just* a supply or *just* an NQT is never helpful. How often do you judge without getting to know the individual or their unique situation?

My year in the cupboard kick-started a deeper understanding of the human behaviours that lead teachers, students and schools towards failure. After spending my own schooling having no clue what education was about, I became a total learning geek. This passion led to me getting excellent results with the most difficult of students (and teachers). Stepping back, observing from all perspectives and never allowing myself to forget those cupboard experiences has shaped my practice. The cupboard began as a reality and became a metaphor for an ongoing practice of human problem solving.

There is a stigma attached to supply teaching. Teachers regard you with suspicion, wondering what is so wrong with you that you can't get a full-time job. Friends often ask me why I still do supply work when I don't have to. I respond by saying that if supply teaching is beneath me, a job that I have risen above, then why do I regularly return home from a day on supply mentally drained? Why does it continue to teach me lessons that I have not learned before? It is worth looking from the perspective of every role in school. Taking on a job that is seen as unimportant or lowly allows me to step into the cupboard and view what it is like to be an NQT, a trainee teacher or a supply teacher. Hearing about these experiences or studying them from afar is not the same as living them.

Taking a cupboard's-eye view of teaching is all about noticing what's actually happening. Harnessing the power of observation can help you to cut through the crap and see what is really going on, leading you to find creative solutions to difficulties and face new problems (there are always more!) with confidence and positivity. When students, teachers or schools are failing, blame, fear and hopelessness are easy get-out clauses, but they don't solve anything. My time in the cupboard has led to a self-reflecting approach that can create solutions no matter how hopeless the situation seems to be. You too can step inside your cupboard and use these reflections to look with fresh eyes on your own daily teaching experiences.

> How are supply teachers treated in your school?

Meeting a new class for the first time can be traumatic. Now imagine that the class is well established, and you are filling in for their favourite teacher. Then allow trauma overload to ensue: 'Where's Miss?' 'What's wrong with her?' 'When will she be back?' Much like the separation anxiety experienced by small children, teenagers don't like to have their much-loved teacher taken away.

When I went from being the favourite to the fill-in, I found myself on a steep learning curve. In my old school, I was well known to most students, but in this school I was just a supply. Most teachers will change schools at one time or another. If you have enjoyed a long(ish) teaching career in one place and then move to another school, you may think that you can walk into any class with your authority and expectations intact. However, like me, you may discover yourself back at the bottom and fighting to regain control and respect.

If you find yourself in a new and scary situation, remember that any problem can be solved through observation and action.

Mrs Terrar

Mrs Terrar knew the power of her name. She had been a teacher for many years, but had retired recently and was doing a stint on supply to boost her retirement fund. She was used to classes cowering in her presence. The mention of her name was enough to get even the most insubordinate kids to tuck their shirt in and stand up straight.

I was the student teacher in the room, and this was supposed to be my lesson, but Mrs Terrar had insisted on starting with her own introduction. She had been missing the fearful faces and didn't want to waste an opportunity to be revered.

'Good morning, children,' she bellowed, clearly enjoying the theatrics. 'My name is Mrs Terrar – Terrar by name and Terrar by nature. You will not want to cross me.' The front row sat wide mouthed listening to this, wondering what the hell was going on and why their trainee teacher (who had been taking them for three weeks now) was sitting in a corner while this terrifying woman took over. The row behind were sniggering at the hilarity of the situation, which did not go down well with Mrs Terrar. Five minutes into the lesson, and two students had been removed and the whole class punished with behaviour points before Mrs Terrar was satisfied that she had dominion over the room. At this point, I was finally allowed to stand up and get on with the lesson.

> Do you look down on student teachers, younger teachers or supply teachers?

Mrs Terrar was new to supply teaching. She was used to having control over her classes and this was all that mattered. She wanted the student teacher in the corner to know who was boss. She wanted the students to respect her as much as she had been respected in her old school. Looking back, I can imagine her gremlins needling at her as she walked into that lesson: 'They are looking at you as if you're just a supply teacher! Don't they know who you are? What you've done? How many years you've been teaching?' Her dictatorial manner led to the behaviour issues at the start of the lesson. She had listened to her teacher gremlins and let them get the better of her because she had a desperate wish to be seen as more than the lowly position she now held. When I began my first posting as a supply teacher, I kept Mrs Terrar in mind.

Solving the problem of being new

The method I describe here is suitable for any teacher who is starting at a new school or who is tasked with stepping in with a class temporarily. It could also be used if you are taking over a class part way through the year, are on long-term supply or in any situation in which the students feel they have ownership over the space. It can help to support the process of building relationships, which in turn leads to higher levels of engagement.

Observation

Once I had established myself as a teacher in my first school, I developed a culture of learning in the classroom. When students entered, they knew the learning had already begun. I would accept nothing less than 100%. It was clear from my first lesson as a supply teacher that a culture of learning could not be forced on a class that had experienced a string of supply teachers. They had already refined their best troublemaking moves. They were practised in the art of disruption without detection. Any attempt to teach was met with disdain – a pack mentality meant they all worked together to diminish my authority. It's us against you, Miss!

Tasked with filling in for a whole month – and knowing they would be primed for a fight – I needed to structure my lessons so that I could observe their learning behaviours and relationships, while also maintaining my authority and control. The more I knew about the way they worked, the more likely it would be that I could form working relationships and convince them that learning was better than anarchy.

I could have chosen to behave like Mrs Terrar and gain control quickly, but I probably would not have gained their respect. The gremlins were whispering in my ear when I faced them: 'Don't they know who you are? They think you're just a supply teacher! Show them what you can do ...' Without this experience, I may never have been able to look back on Mrs Terrar with understanding. But I understood now.

> When you have a problem class, how do you deal with it?

Solution

My question was: *how can I quickly establish a working relationship with a class I have just met?* My plan was to quickly evaluate the circumstances of the class – who they were, the space we had to work with, their past experiences, their abilities and any other information that I could get my hands on so that I could engage them as swiftly as possible in learning. I was armed with the school's behaviour for learning policy and knew the expectations in terms of tackling poor behaviour. Of course, this is not what I say to students when we first meet. I don't open the conversation by telling them that I know their school's behaviour policy inside out and can make sure that they are punished for any transgressions, which would be more likely to upset them than settle them down! However, I do have this information in mind for my own confidence.

> How often do you evaluate your lessons, looking for ways to improve?

Testing the solution

My first supply posting was in a school devoted to the five R's (reasoning, resilience, reflectiveness, resourcefulness and respect). These five R's were all over the school, in posters and on planners, so I knew the students would be familiar with them. Schools often have foci – such as personal learning and thinking skills (PLTS), or their own version – so it is worth finding out what the culture is and using it to your advantage.

I set the lesson up so that all of the information the students needed was visible. I projected the following title onto the board: 'Your controlled assessment preparation.' The emphasis was on 'your'. This was not my class. Their success depended on how well they dealt with their teacher's absence. Context was key; I had been given some background information on the class so I knew where they were in their learning and where they needed to be. This was clearly not a filler task designed to keep them quiet but a continuation of necessary learning.

I made clear in my written instructions, also projected onto the board, exactly what they had to do and how they should go about doing it. My goal was to enable them to make a positive choice to engage. They had been learning about Shakespeare for a few weeks, so the task I set them was to gather information on three key areas of *Romeo and Juliet* – the themes, structure and storyline. They were given blank A4 booklets in which to write down the information. It was important that both myself and the students were enabled – I wanted them to be able to work independently so that I could observe their behaviour. The key to success was ensuring that my instructions were clear and that the necessary resources were accessible, so the learning could begin promptly.

I had placed envelopes around the room containing printed information on each of the three research areas, and the students were given a time limit of three lessons for the task (roughly one lesson per key area). I informed them that if they demonstrated any of the five R's they would be rewarded. Off they went.

Observing how the students went about the task enabled me to find out about them as individuals, and therefore plan more effective learning in subsequent lessons. What were their names? Who worked well with whom? What engaged them? What annoyed them? Did they have a culture of learning or a culture of apathy? What did they want to achieve when they left school? What were their thoughts about English? Which other lessons did they talk about? What additional information could I find out about them – their interests and hobbies? I used this intelligence to plan support, challenge and engagement into later lessons. I dealt with any poor behaviour quickly and quietly. Any faltering and this lesson would not work at all.

During lesson one, the students asked lots of questions about the task. This meant they needed my help, which I hoped would mean they would be willing to listen to my answers, hopefully lessening the chance for confrontation. I had prepared some examples in anticipation of any misunderstandings.

As I had planned to promote the school focus on the five R's, I had stocked up on five different-coloured sticky dots. I awarded the stickers to students who were demonstrating effective learning, calmly explaining what they had done to deserve the sticker. This had the knock-on effect of students copying positive behaviours and fewer students behaving negatively. Stickers have a strange effect – no matter the age of the student, they all want one!

Extra credit questions on each of the research areas were introduced part way through the second lesson. If the students worked hard, they would feel able to engage with and learn from the extra work. They could choose to answer these questions to show that they were reasoning through their research, as well as performing the research itself. I set the questions at three levels (gold, silver and bronze) so the students could choose their entry level into this work.

Review

Within three lessons, a class of aggressive and unresponsive teenagers were no longer apathetic or avoiding work. They were searching for meaning and making meaning for themselves. The students were enabled to work as everything was easily accessible. They were engaged in positive learning behaviours through a praise tool already familiar to them (the five R's). I was most pleased by the lack of confrontation, how I had managed to develop an understanding of their specific context, which led to a culture of learning that did not involve me imposing myself too heavily on them, and that the students recognised what I could do for them.

If you ever need to take over another teacher's class, this approach of observation, solution, testing the solution and review could help you to avoid lost learning too.

When you find yourself faced with a difficult situation, take a step back and prepare to make it count for your development as a professional. Explore where the students are in reality. What are their starting points? Where are the problems? Where are the strengths? What has happened? What do they like? What do they dislike? The more questions you ask, the more likely it is that you will take the right action to move the class forward.

Set up lessons that allow you to take a step back and watch your students' behaviours. Don't allow your emotions to cloud your understanding of what is really going on. Observe their relationships, their actions and what makes them tick. Be on the lookout for information that will enable you to capture their attention for learning.

Then take action: use what you have learned and turn it into a plan. Be creative! Not everything will work first time. Sometimes you will need to return to the drawing board and rethink. Again, don't react with emotion when your plans don't play out as you had hoped. Take this opportunity to review what you have learned from the situation, re-evaluate and try out something new.

Chapter 8

I'LL HAVE TO WORK LATE TONIGHT – WE'VE HAD 'THE CALL'

> Teaching is not a game to be played only when the adults are looking. The children are not pieces that can be moved around to suit your needs. Their lives can be changed in inspirational classrooms. They can also be scarred, broken and turned off by the other players.

Have you ever come across a colleague getting excellent feedback when you know their classes are terrible? Somehow they manage to pull it out of the bag for an inspection or a lesson observation even though their day-to-day practice is second-rate. There is something about inspections and lesson observations that makes people work in a way that is not typical for them. Shouldn't we all find a way of working that we can keep up all of the time?

When that phone call came at a school where I was working as a classroom assistant, everyone went into a strange sort of meltdown – or wind up, I'm not sure. Teachers stayed up all night marking books that hadn't been touched all year; new and improved lesson planning sheets that had never been used before were stacked high on the staffroom table for all to use (or else); teachers began greeting students at classroom doors for the first time ever; teachers even had jobs for me and my fellow classroom assistants to do in lessons. Everyone worked themselves to the point of exhaustion.

The poor rating came as a shock to everyone. How could the school have been judged so badly when everyone had worked so hard (for two days)? The habit of putting on a show for visitors is all too common. Many teachers put in a bit of effort, dazzle in a one-off lesson observation, and then pack away their resources and continue to pour the syllabus into their kids' ears. Not all schools operate in this way, but many do.

A member of the leadership team had been graded as unsatisfactory in their lesson – this was at a time when Ofsted still used graded observations as standard. This same senior manager was the lead for most internal inspections. How could we look up to him when he had been looked down on by the powers that be? Simple! The head teacher took up a clipboard and observed the leader again. Within one week of getting a poor judgement, he had turned it around and been classified as outstanding. Nothing to see here, minions. Move on. Forget what you heard. Rubbish! The insiders knew (but wouldn't dare communicate that to the leaders) and no amount of duplicity could explain away the lies. If there wasn't an us and them culture before, there certainly was now.

Honing your skills as a teacher means working hard and learning your craft. It means that some lessons will go well and some will go badly. You should not be too quick to congratulate yourself or put yourself out of the job you love. It is a learning process – a process that, even when you have mastered it, will throw up new obstacles and problems that you must use your skill and creativity to overcome.

None of this happens in a one-off lesson observation. And it certainly doesn't happen if you get your mate to tell everyone that you are a good teacher. It won't happen if you are persistently battered with the 'unsatisfactory' stick either. Collaboration, fair observation, skilled human behaviours and learning over time are all ways in which we can improve. Fake observations do nothing but annoy people!

Can teach, won't teach

School inspections are exhausting because everyone is under the microscope. You want to show yourself at your best, and that is understandable. However, if your best is something that you only pull out for an inspection, this cannot be right. As a classroom assistant, I sat in the same drama class with 9Z3 each week. The teacher was strong and respected, so my 9Z3-ers rarely messed about. Unfortunately, they were not his priority and so his strengths as a teacher did not shine through. There was always an incident on the way into the room. Someone would shove the person in front; someone would sneeze when the teacher had asked for silence; someone would drop a book … It didn't matter what it was, but it always had the same effect: 'Right! No drama again this week. You can't be trusted. Get your books out and read for the whole hour. Maybe next week you will learn …' They never did. This was a weekly occurrence that even I, as an unqualified nobody, could see was a ruse for the teacher to avoid ever having to teach the class.

I'd been excited when I first saw drama on my timetable. It had been one of my favourite subjects until Year 9, although my poor behaviour in other classes had led to me not being allowed to take it as a GCSE. But that didn't stop me from taking part in school plays and running the weekly whole-school assemblies. In this school, drama seemed to be regarded as an add-on for English rather than as a subject in its own right. And the drama teacher seemed to see it as a free period for getting his marking done.

> Do you save your best lessons for observations?

Then the inspectors arrived … 9Z3 were lined up, waiting for 'the incident' to occur, and had their books out ready for boredom when out the teacher came. He had on a clown's hat and invited the students to guess what the lesson was going to be about. In a shocked disbelief, the class gave him the answers he wanted. 'Circus skills?' 'Clowns?' 'Fun?' they answered one by one, waiting patiently with their hands up, as if this was the way we began every lesson.

Then I saw her – clipboard in hand, glasses poised on the end of her nose. The inspector was in the room!

The lesson was awesome. The children learned about humour in plays and explored what jokes make us laugh the most. They even had an opportunity to try out some stand-up on each other. Everything was perfect, and I'm pretty sure the knowing smile on the inspector's face suggested that this was an outstanding performance. The problem was that once the inspectors had given their judgement, I never experienced a drama lesson like it again. The clown hat was off and the corridor incidents returned. The lesson plans stopped pouring into my pigeon hole, and I was put back in the cupboard again.

> Do you see the value in your relationships with classes?

I felt powerless. This teacher knew exactly how to make a lesson come to life, but chose not to, week after week. During my early days in education, I did nothing to change the terrible teaching that I observed. If I knew then what I know now, I would have taken steps to challenge this teacher's behaviours. However, at the time I did not have the knowledge or the confidence. Despite the hopelessness, my observations did at least lead to better outcomes for my own students as I grew as an educator.

A mantra that came out of this crazy inspection stays with me: 'You are always being observed by the children in your class.' Your students are always watching you. Treat them as your official observers. Imagine that they go directly to the head teacher after each lesson and give them a breakdown of how you are helping them to improve, how they feel in your lesson and how you behave as a teacher. Would that change your practice? You can't fake every lesson, and nor should you. Truly outstanding teaching means doing the best you can for your students every single day.

It all went wrong but nothing's broken

Doing the best we can doesn't always look like perfection. Knowing our subject, our students and our learning outcomes is a great starting point for great teaching. But we can plan every second of our lessons using this knowledge and experience, and things can still go wrong. We are teaching human beings, so even if we have taught the same lesson fifty times, we can't predict what the students will do.

11X1 and I had known each other for three years as class and teacher. I knew their strengths and they knew that if I was teaching a lesson, it had purpose. That is not a trick you can pull out of the bag for an observation. It takes time to get to know a class. It takes high-quality assessment for learning. It means ensuring that every lesson is meaningful, so they come to expect that lessons are worth paying attention to every time. Not every lesson will go according to plan, but over time a team relationship is formed. We all knew our roles and we all played them well for the good of the team.

One day, a group of Scottish teachers came to visit. The trip had been planned in advance and 11X1 were the class they were coming to see me teach. At a recent TeachMeet, I had learned a game that I just couldn't wait to try out with the class, so I set it up for the lesson with the visiting teachers. Alas, the game fell flat on its face! It just didn't work. The class and I openly discussed the issues with how the game was intended to work and what we could do to improve it next time. The game was then left and we moved on to the next part of the lesson. No dramas – no worries.

The visitors then dispersed around the room, chatting to the students. They were able to answer questions about what they were doing, why they were doing it and how it fitted into the bigger picture of their learning. Their answers had not been rehearsed. Nothing was faked. This was the culture of our classroom. I never asked whether this lesson would have been rated outstanding or not. Outstanding means nothing if it is a one-off grade based on a one-time visit. Outstanding comes from my students who experience my lessons every day. Only they have the experience to judge.

Try this!

The relationship you have with your classes is vital. Do you dare ask them to be the judge of your lessons? Be warned: reflecting on their learning will only work if you have already established a good rapport with the students. A class that is out to destroy you (like many I experienced during my time on supply) is unlikely to give you good, honest feedback.

If you do have a good relationship with your class, and you do dare to canvass the student voice on your lessons, try regularly ending your lessons with a short survey on how you could improve the learning for them. I used to do this before each half-term to give me a chance to work on any improvements. In this way, I have learned things about my teaching that only a student could tell me. This has helped me to create a well-balanced working relationship. It has also allowed me to model that we are all learners in our classroom.

Here are some questions to choose from to get feedback from your class:

+ What do you enjoy most about our lessons? Why?

+ What do you enjoy least? Why?

+ What is the one thing you would change about our classroom? Why?

+ Do you find it easy to understand when I give instructions? Why? Why not?

+ Do you find my visual examples useful? Why? Why not?

+ Can you read my handwriting?

+ Do you always know how to improve? Why? Why not?

- Are there things that you find useful in other lessons that we could use too?

- What was our best lesson this half-term? Why?

- Do you feel comfortable answering questions in our lessons?

- Do you feel safe in our lessons?

- Do you know what is expected of you in our lessons?

- Are the procedures in our classroom useful? Why? Why not?

You could concentrate on a particular line of questioning each half-term. For example, after the first half-term, you could ask questions about rules, procedures and safety. You would then make this your focus of improvement in the second half-term. You could review this regularly through discussion and, if everyone was happy that the environment was just right, you could then move on to the role of direct instruction and how to ensure clarity.

Chapter 9

WHAT'S THE POINT?

> Learning should be purposeful beyond the final exam. The magic parts of most subjects don't always appear on the exam and life is not compartmentalised into subjects. Passing the exam should come as standard when proper learning has taken place and the students are confident and knowledgeable, *not* because they have been drilled with the correct answers.

Do you ever ask yourself, 'Why am I teaching them that?' Teachers frequently complain about not having time to explore the more interesting aspects of their subject. Lessons take place every day in schools in which the teacher is either cramming content for the exam or giving students pointless time-filling tasks. Once children reach Year 2, it is apparently time to knuckle down and get their test techniques mastered. By the time you have thoroughly turned all of the kids off learning with boring and repetitive practice – which has no purpose other than to get them through the exam – how long do you think it will take for them to forget their learning and hope they never come across it again? Is it possible to devise stimulating and challenging lessons, while still making sure your students pass their exam?

Your students (and you) are living through tough times. Social media is making a mockery of identity. Mental health issues are prevalent throughout society at all ages. War, terrorism and climate change dominate the news. Young people aren't stupid. They know that the adults have no clue how to fix these crises. They are surrounded by chaos and yet they go to school only to be drilled about seemingly irrelevant facts.

I persistently asked my maths teacher why I had to learn maths. His response: 'It's for the exam.' As I wanted to be a mad scientist at the time, passing my maths exam was not my top priority, and so I didn't pay attention and failed. Had the teacher asked me about my hopes and dreams, he could have made a link with my reality to give maths more purpose (it's one of the STEM subjects, after all, and would have been crucial in any science career). But our relationship wasn't important to him, and I knew it. Maths facts could have been taught in a way that supported my confidence in communication, problem solving, reflecting on mistakes, becoming a better teamworker – the list really is endless – but they weren't. Drill, drill, drill … dull, dull, dull … fail!

Facts are important. Without knowledge, you can't think creatively and imaginatively. Is there a way to create knowledgeable learners, but also give them an understanding of the real world – how to navigate it, create within it, solve huge global problems and live happy lives? Of course there is! However, in the majority of schools in which I have worked, this is not happening yet.

League tables and exam results dominate the school agenda. The curriculum is condensed into practising skills and content that will be examined. Each half-term students take part in assessments that check how closely they are performing to expected points on a trajectory. The grade that students are expected to achieve in their final year of school has often been decided during their primary years. Exam results at age 11 create a pathway through to Year 11, so don't you dare have an off day at primary school! Extra classes are put on after school and at weekends to drill the same exam content. In departmental meetings, teaching and learning are pushed aside to concentrate on scrutinising the data extracted from the latest mock exam.

Teachers don't feel like they have the time to be creative because that would detract from teaching to the test. The thinking goes, 'If it's not on the exam, why would I teach it?' Teachers' pay is linked to their students' outcomes, so fear of failure is driving them more than it is driving most students. This is a problem that can be solved, as long as we stop doing stupid things and start looking for solutions.

Time use

One of the worst lessons I have ever sat through started with fifteen minutes of free time and ended with fifteen minutes of free time – if the students behaved. The whole lesson was only fifty minutes long! Although they wanted the free time, the students were clearly bored. Meanwhile, the teacher, who was using the free time as a tool to gain their respect, could not see that it was creating chaos. The lesson in-between consisted of them heading to the computers, switching them on, finding a software program and playing with it. Would they remember this program afterwards? How would it support their literacy or numeracy? How would the program help them to be successful in life? All of these questions were left unanswered as the children scrambled out of the room for break.

One lesson can't tell you everything, but I have observed enough to know that pointless lessons happen quite often, especially in the years when students aren't being examined. Every lesson – no matter what the subject or the age of the students – has the potential to be purposeful without detracting from high-quality results.

This was an extreme case. Not all teachers fritter away so much 'free time', but all schools waste time in different ways. One school I worked in had a scheduled life skills lesson for the whole school each week. Time spent learning about real-life issues – a great idea! Perhaps they would learn about handling social media, find out about mental health issues or explore terrorism and its causes. The programme was well put together and did touch on many of these matters, with each year group given age-appropriate tasks to help them develop skills for life.

> Have you ever complained that there is not enough time to teach GCSE, but doled out time-filling Key Stage 3 tasks?

However, what I observed in practice was teachers using this time to catch up on marking while their tutor groups chatted, leisurely filling in worksheets. Many students busied themselves in emptying recycling bins so they could meet their mates from other tutor groups and wander the corridors. There were a few GCSE catch-up classes going on too – more exam drilling! This was not time well spent. As a tutor, what would you do? As a leader, what would you do? As a student, what would you do?

Both of these are examples of time used poorly. Timetables need to be planned carefully in both primary and secondary schools. Catch-up classes should be reserved for those students who really need them. If this isn't the reason they're being scheduled, then something is going very wrong. In my first book, *Manglish*, I detail how we can organise the curriculum to maximise the time spent on learning and avoid cognitive overload.[1] Time does not have to be wasted. But time does need to be spent rethinking how we organise the curriculum to get the best learning results.

Observation

During my time on supply, one class taught me how letting students down can be a whole-school effort. This class were given the title 'Stage Not Age', meaning they were behind their peers in their learning. The students had a mixture of moderate learning difficulties and behavioural issues, and so had been segregated to give them extra attention, and specific content and skills development geared towards their learning needs, right? Wrong. In reality, they were not expected to achieve anything – they were being babysat. Lessons consisted of colouring in and damage control.

If we collectively expect nothing from students, what do we think they are going to achieve? That's right, nothing. The students were aware of their ranking in the school's (not so) cleverly thought out streaming system. They might not have known much, but they knew that 1 comes at the top and that they appeared at the bottom (just like my 9Z3 class who knew that Z comes a long way after A in the alphabet). These students know that they have ended their

---

1   See Lisa Jane Ashes, *Manglish: Bringing Maths and English Together Across the Curriculum* (Carmarthen: Independent Thinking Press, 2014).

primary years way behind their peers and have often been turned off learning at a very young age thanks to early failures.

If you dare to believe that these students can learn, the chances are you are on your own. They are already used to the easy way – to poor behaviour providing more satisfaction than learning ever could. During one lesson, a boy with a reading age of less than 3 – drugged up on stimulants for his attention deficit hyperactivity disorder and high on blue pop from breaktime – became overwrought. I'd dared to have high expectations, dared to set a challenging task, dared to hope that they could achieve more than a spider diagram today. The howling took me by surprise. He was always noisy but this was something else. He fell writhing to the floor. I knew learning could be tough, but had I actually popped his brain? I couldn't get him to respond. The wailing was piercing and brought in two other teachers from adjoining classrooms. When we finally got him to stand, we saw the blood trickling from his hands. He had ripped out his own fingernails on the corner of a door in a fit of rage. This lesson had been a failure.

When a culture of zero expectations is engrained so deeply that high expectations can have such a catastrophic effect, a collective effort is required. One teacher's culture shift might eventually pay off, but every teacher recognising the problem and working together to solve it is more likely to have the desired effect.

> Has a lesson you've designed ever affected your students' emotions negatively?

A solution-focused question was in order, which was: *how can we show these students that there is a purpose to learning and give them the skills they need to engage?*

Solution

As a main English teacher in this setting, I had a full timetable. It was not possible for me to follow these students around the school. Instead, I gathered together their teachers and the head of literacy to explore what was going wrong. We met after school during a period of whole-school training. We discussed what strategies were already being used in lessons and how teachers were currently coping with the demands of this group. We all put forward potential solutions to the problem. It was clear that their teachers did not think this group could achieve much more than colouring in. However, by refocusing on the solution-focused question, we began to think about ways to work together and combat the low expectations.

The class were experiencing the same basic timetable as the rest of the school. They would have six lessons every day, each lesson very different from the last. In *The Hidden Lives of Learners*, Graham Nuthall suggests that students must come into contact with new information or skills at least three times consecutively before it can become embedded for life.[2] But that applies to an 'ordinary' student without specific learning needs. These students were 'extraordinary' and would probably require even more repetition. That said, their attention spans were probably not up to the hours of repetition required, and so the behaviour problems would kick right back in. They were getting their reward from impressing their peers rather than from learning. We needed to use this information to create a solution.

It was agreed that literacy and learning skills should be the thread that tied all the lessons together. In my English lessons, they would focus on reading skills and the teachers of their other subjects would support this by finding out about these skills and how they were taught, and then applying them in their lessons. For example, I taught the students how to identify key points in a text and deduce their meaning. I began with images, asking them to identify everything they could see in a picture. From what they had identified, I

2   Graham Nuthall, *The Hidden Lives of Learners* (Wellington: New Zealand Council for Educational Research Press, 2007).

then asked them what they could deduce. If their geography teacher wanted them to learn about volcanoes, for example, she would similarly use images and vocabulary to help them identify and then explore volcanoes. The history teacher would employ the same method to teach them about the First World War, and so on across all their subjects. The students began to see that the skill of reading could allow them to access learning across the curriculum. They were not overloaded with new learning strategies, but used the same strategies over and over again to master the basic skills.

We also introduced a PLTS log to encourage students to adopt positive learning behaviours – such as creative thinking, independent enquiry, managing themselves and so on – across their subjects, and be rewarded for this. Their teachers would recognise when they had displayed a good learning behaviour (e.g. working well in a team), praise them publicly for their efforts, make it clear what was being praised and record the praise with a sticker in the teamwork section of their log.

After years of underachievement, they were getting no satisfaction from learning. It was difficult, vague and meandering. The PLTS log aimed to highlight good learning behaviours in real time – to get the students feeling satisfaction in the moment and to feel rewarded by their experiences in class. A blank example of the log can be found in the Resource Cupboard.

> Do you know what your students are learning across the curriculum or just in your own lessons?

You can do anything!

Start by getting the right skills

- Keep this log with you in every lesson
- Practise your personal learning and thinking skills
- Get signatures from teachers when they recognise you have shown skill
- Get rewards for your effort

'If you think you can …
You can!'

– With great effort comes great reward

My PLTS Log

Passport to success

Name:

Class:

Aim:

Creative **Thinker**	Independent **Enquirer**	Reflective **Learner**
Team **Player**	Effective **Participant**	Self-**Manager**

Testing the solution

Students carried their PLTS logs with them from lesson to lesson and placed them visibly on their desks. The tasks were set at an appropriate level so that it felt like a desirable difficulty – not too hard and not too easy.[3] They had to be assignments that took effort, but not so much that their fingernails were in danger! Teachers had to think carefully about what the students already knew and what they needed to do to improve. They then had to set the challenge just right. Use the riddles that follow to help you understand more about desirable difficulties.

Try this!

I use the following problems as a metaphor for planning lessons at an appropriate level of difficulty. Have a go at each riddle and see how it makes you feel.

Riddle 1

You are in an empty room. You have a candle, some matches and a box of drawing pins. They are ordinary in every way. You have to fix the candle so that it is five feet above the ground without having to hold it there. You have tried melting wax and sticking it to the wall, but that didn't work. How are you going to do it?[4]

---

3 The phrase 'desirable difficulty' was coined by Robert A. Bjork in Institutional Impediments to Effective Training. In Daniel Druckman and Robert A. Bjork (eds), *Learning, Remembering, Believing: Enhancing Human Performance* (Washington, DC: National Academies Press, 1994), pp. 295–306.

4 This riddle, originally named Duncker's candle problem, was created in 1945 by Karl Duncker as a creativity test. I have not included the answer here, although it is readily available on the Internet. I recommend that you attempt to solve it first – it will feel good when you come up with the solution!

Riddle 2

What has hands that can't clap? (*Hint: tick-tock!*)

Riddle 3

Why is the distant universe so homogeneous, when the Big Bang theory seems to predict larger measurable antistrophes of the night sky than those observed? Cosmological inflation is generally the accepted solution, but are other possible explanations – such as a variable speed of light – more appropriate?

How you solve each riddle will depend on the templates that have been created in your mind by your experiences. If you believe that you are no good at riddles, you may have avoided even attempting the first one; however, given time, most people crack it. You can visualise all of the elements, so you can experiment with ideas until you find a solution that works. This is a desirable difficulty. The second riddle is too easy. It gives us very little satisfaction because we can work it out quickly and are left waiting to move on. Unless you have a degree in physics, the third riddle (an unsolved physics problem) is unlikely to have held your attention for long. Therefore, riddles two and three are undesirable.

A desirable difficulty is the 'sweet spot' for teaching. We need to know what our students already know and set the level of challenge appropriately. They need to be able to wrestle with any new information presented to solve the problem for themselves and thereby gain the sense of satisfaction that comes from learning.

As they worked, I looked out for the positives. These students would recognise insincerity if they saw it, so I needed to identify genuine learning behaviours. As soon as I spotted them, I was quick to praise exactly what I had seen. For example, student A was solving a problem by creating an unprompted diagram. 'That's excellent!' I'd say. 'That's what independent enquirers do. They find their own methods to solve problems.' I would place a simple sticker in the 'independent enquirer' section of their log and move on. Student B has noticed that student A got a sticker for trying to solve the problem with a diagram. Student B adopts a similar method. 'Great!' I say to student B. 'You have shown the skill of being reflective. You have reflected on student A's approach and are trying this out for yourself.' They would get a sticker in the 'reflective learner' section of their log.

The students were rewarded with a sticker for positive learning behaviours, but more importantly they got a sense of satisfaction from the skills they were demonstrating. Over time, their logs filled up with stickers and they could reflect on which skills they were best at and which skills they needed to spend more time developing. Their learning behaviours were also improving. As a result, I was able to up the challenge little by little as they began to feel a sense of achievement from their learning.

The log was taken from class to class to provide a link between subjects. It was a tangible record for the students that they were building skills that would lead to them becoming better learners. It demonstrated how they were growing with each task they completed. With a collective effort across the curriculum, they began to feel a sense of pride in their work in all lessons. Even the child with fewer fingernails began to see the purpose in his learning after a short period of being rewarded for the positives.

At the end of each half-term, the student who had made the most progress in their learning behaviours was rewarded with a prize from the Box of Awe and Wonder. (Dr Matthew McFall had donated the box as a prize at the Independent Thinking Big i Foundation Ball. I had to have it! It is filled with curiosities – old dice, yo-yos, shoe wings and adventure books, to name but a few of the assorted bits of fun in there.) The logs were then reset to zero. Each month the students were given a fresh start, a chance to grow and learn.

Our lessons now had a purpose far beyond damage control. The students were learning to be learners, and we loved it!

Try this!

Although the end goal is for our students to pass their exams, the real goal is to educate them. If all we do is fill children with information for the exam, never deviating from that purpose, we are not educating them. We are programming them.

Take the what, how and why test regularly to explore the purpose of your lessons. Take any task you have set this week and ask:

What?

+ What am I teaching the students to do?

+ Is it a skill?

+ Is it understanding something they did not understand before?

+ Is it a life lesson?

+ Is it part of the bigger picture?

+ Is it just filling time with a topic that you have to cover because it's on the exam? (If so, bin it! Time for a rethink.)

How?

+ How will students be learning this?

+ Are they active in their learning? Are they being taught to question for themselves/find the answer/explore alternative solutions/do something that will support their learning?

+ Are they passive? If yes, are they passive because it is the easiest way to get the information across? (If so, bin it! Time for a rethink.)

Why?

+ Why are they learning this? What is the purpose of learning this for them?

+ Will they practise a useful life skill?

+ Will they use this information in the bigger picture?

+ Will they be able to work easier knowing this?

+ Will this information only be useful in their exam? (If so, bin it! Time for a rethink.)

Review

Lessons without purpose are pointless. You might as well watch a DVD for an hour and waste your time properly. Schools can be so busy attempting to play the game that they don't devote sufficient time to the bigger picture. It's as if teachers and leaders are juggling plates while running on a treadmill. They are so afraid that they will fall off and the plates will smash that they keep going blindly onwards, exhausted and doing a substandard job.

How can we create real purpose in lessons? The answer to this question will depend on your individual school and your individual circumstances. You can't create and execute a solution without turning off the treadmill, putting down the plates and creating time. Just like the teacher who gives their free time to non-exam classes, while complaining that there is no time to cover the GCSE course, there is time – it's just being wasted.

Writing a child off because of their ability, but then forcing them to stay in education until they are 18 is just wrong! Why do we do this to them? Either we help them to find a way or we need alternative routes to success.

Chapter 10

I CAN'T HELP THEM ALL

As an undergraduate, aged 19, I entered a school again. It was an inner-city primary school, and they were used to students coming in for this unit. 'Students into Schools' was an easy module. Turn up, help out and then evaluate what you had done in an essay. I could do that. It was my very first glimpse behind the curtain. The staffroom, that once mystical place, was now opened up to me. It stunk! Not just of coffee but of conversations that made me sick. 'What can we get *her* to do this afternoon?' they asked each other (her was me), as if I wasn't there. 'Charlie and Jake are too stupid for SATs. She can play games with them.'

Most teachers want to support their students. However, the 'too stupid' conversation was not a one-off. Often, the problem is not the student; it is the teacher's view of the student. Those students who need the most support can be a job too far for the overworked teacher. Secondary school teachers have to pick up the pieces for children like Charlie and Jake. Imagine that you have been labelled as stupid at primary school and are left behind as your peers soar ahead. Everyone has got their end-of-year results and you know that yours are way below everyone else's. Are you feeling the joy of education? Are you thinking (aged 11) that you can achieve whatever you want to achieve, or are you looking for somewhere else to fit in?

Observation

In my experience, Year 7 classes are the easiest to teach as the children are new to the school and have not yet developed the confidence to defy their teachers. Then there's Charlie. He's not even got into the classroom before he's had a fight and then refused to start your lesson. Charlie is looked up to by his peers.

He challenges his teachers and messes about when the teacher is talking. He fails to see, or care, about the consequences of his actions. And always looks like he is having a good time when he is being defiant.

Now consider Charlie's background. He was the lowest achieving student in his cohort at primary school. With a reading age of 6, he is held back in most subjects as he just can't access the material. He had six weeks off school with a broken ankle during his final primary year and it was deemed that there was no point in him catching up – best just hope he can plod on. Charlie hates school but he doesn't hate people. His way of fitting in is to be a legend to his peers, and there is no way he is giving that up.

> Do you ever let children fail?

Then there's Jamal. He's in the same class as Charlie. His reading is better but he is not that much further ahead. You haven't got to know Jamal as well as the other students because, at least once a week, he doesn't turn up. Jamal is a persistent absentee. His parents give in when he tells them he has a headache, a stomach ache, a toe ache. He has gained access to a time-out card and he is going to use it! Jake is the least of your worries; all you have to do is catch him up with his peers.

What about Aisha? You have barely got the instructions out of your mouth before Aisha chimes in: 'I don't get it.' 'What am I supposed to do again?' 'I don't understand.' You know she is lacking in self-confidence – she has been the same from the start of the year. Your lessons have been slowed down because she never, ever gets it first time. This makes the others laugh and you have a hunch that she is winding you up.

> Is differentiation something you only do for observations?

Then there's Sophie who can't seem to stay awake, Desiree who constantly needs the toilet, Tyrone who has dyspraxia, Arun who has dyslexia, Peter who is on a managed move and bloody Kate who, on top of all of these problems, is always finished early and wants more work. This Year 7 class isn't the dream team you had hoped for – surely, you can't help them all! Best just to stick to the ones who you know can be successful, right? If you get some work out of the others, that's a bonus. When the results come out, you can always explain to your head of department that you couldn't help them all. They'll understand.

But will Charlie understand the purpose of education when you and your colleagues leave him behind? How will Jamal feel about school when he looks back on it? Will Aisha ever get it if you don't help her? Will Kate achieve her full potential if you ignore her pleas for extra work? And will the others understand that you had too much on your plate to make a plan to ensure that their time with you was purposeful? That they have wasted a year of learning because they are seen as having no hope? Can you picture these children in the future, or do you just see them as they are today? Once they have left your care, do you wonder where they will go or what they will do? Our education years shape who we are; if you have been identified as hopeless because a teacher can't help everyone, how will that shape your future?

Solution

How can I effectively support and challenge all learners without exhausting myself? When we are overwhelmed by the number of differing needs in our classes, the default is to help those who can be helped and write off the others as no-hopers. The classroom is split between those who can and those who can't, with the teacher preferring to help only those who can.

The solution is to make the classroom into a differentiation haven by getting prepared and taking control. No child should be left behind. If a child has been in your class for the last twelve months and you have made no impact on their education, then you are the one with the problem. Don't allow it to get to this point. Here are some suggestions to make differentiation manageable.

Assign your roles

Charlie has failed – and been failed – in so much. In order to feel like he has achieved, he needs to be the centre of negative attention. Prepare a series of roles before you have even met your class. Assume there will be a Charlie in there somewhere. What roles could you assign him and others to make them feel they are in control of their learning in this space?

Prepare your drawers

For the children with dyslexia, dyspraxia or any other specific educational need, fill your drawers with resources to support them, which you have bought in or created. You may have a child with sight difficulties; no problem, you have a magnifying glass in your drawers. Dyslexia? You have some sheets of coloured Perspex for them to read through to improve their speed and comprehension. Dyspraxia? You have some pencil grips and sloping rests already prepared. Don't wait to find out the needs of the child and then rush around looking for resources. Think smart and be prepared.

> Are your displays simply wallpaper or do you use them creatively?

Example ready!

Aisha doesn't get it. She takes up class time with constant questions. You need to have some examples ready for her if your explanation won't do. If you are teaching the same thing, year in, year out, you will find that certain misconceptions crop up again and again. Your verbal explanations may be getting through to some children, so create some visual examples ready for the next Aisha who comes your way. In this way, she can work out more for herself and you will have more time to concentrate on those who need one-to-one support.

Super stuck wall

For the persistent absentee, attending school can get tedious when they have no idea what everyone else has been learning about. Prepare to catch them up quick with a super stuck wall. Gather together notes, PowerPoint slides, written questions, reading material and so on in dated folders. Attach the folders, which should be clearly labelled, to the wall so they are easily accessible to the students. For example, you could have folders with key information about each strand of the topic you are teaching, or folders with instructions on how to do something specific. Direct the absentee to the folder that is right for them and give them time to draw level with their classmates. Perhaps set the catch-up work as homework or let them reflect alone. If you give them a little space, they will feel less stressed about coming to your lesson and will be more likely to catch up. If you get into the habit of creating a super stuck wall, it won't add to your workload – you will just get used to filing notes in the relevant folders and allowing the children to catch up when necessary. It is not just Jamal who will have a day off, so you will be supporting many more children besides.

Challenge corner

Kate won't remain interested for long if she finds her learning too easy. A challenge corner is perfect when you have a child who finishes quickly and is desperate to move on. It should be filled with resources to enable them to learn more about a topic or think about it in a different way. This need not be a challenge for you, although you will need to change and adapt the material for different lessons.

For example, you might have been teaching about glaciated regions and all of the children are filling in the features. Kate finishes before the rest of the class, but you are still helping other students who have not quite grasped it yet, so you ask her to go to the challenge corner and see what she would like to work on next. In the challenge corner, she finds three options. The first is a book about glaciated regions and the challenge is to 'read about one glaciated region and write about the features you have been learning about in reality'. The second option is to 'choose a glaciated region and then write about and describe your journey as you walk through it – ensuring that you name the features and describe them as if you were really there'. The third option is to 'create an acronym that will enable you to remember all of the features you have learned and which you can teach to the others later'.

Kate now has several choices that will keep her learning about the same topic, but also allow her to develop her understanding. She is unlikely to finish all three tasks but they are varied enough to avoid her becoming bored with more-of-the-same learning.

Information station

Prepare your information station with articles, books and images – anything you can get your hands on that might provide further interesting information to your knowledge-thirsty students. This area is not just for Kate – this is an area for all. The students can spend a little time exploring this information when you are helping someone else and they are waiting to speak to you. If you label the material by section, their question might even be answered by a little further reading.

Testing the solution

Your classroom can be updated as you go. Continually ask yourself what works well and what doesn't. Add to your resources as new challenges arise. Look at the methods you employ to get the students using the space and enjoy creating something spectacular. Use the students to help you update the space. Your students are the primary users of this material, so their opinions can be really useful in exploring what works well and what needs to be updated and improved. Ask them! You can also work alongside colleagues to observe systems and materials in action. Use their observations, comments and ideas to update and improve your methods.

Whatever you do, don't forget that you are testing a solution. By observing your solution in practice, developing and tweaking it as you go, you could create something spectacular that could solve issues way beyond your classroom. The awesome power that problem solving can have on your practice is in your hands. Test as many solutions as you can and keep your classroom moving forward.

Review

Support drawers, a super stuck wall, a challenge corner, an information station – it might sound like a lot of work. Well, let's be honest, it is a lot of work to begin with. However, the effort will pay off when you have a classroom that is primed for learning. In the long term, you are making your job easier because differentiation will part of your classroom furniture. You are prepared!

This way of working will enable you to spend time with the children most in need of your help and attention, while the others can be directed quickly towards independent support. The children who most need your help and attention are likely to be the ones who, in a traditional classroom setting, are usually kicked out first. They are the noisiest and the most irritating. If you can create a learning space that enables you to help them onto the ladder, without damaging anyone else's education, you are winning at your job.

During the last week of any term, review your space and prepare yourself for the term to come using your reflections. Keep the brilliant stuff, adapt the mediocre and get rid of anything that doesn't work for you and your learners. Then, when you are ready, take a nice long break – you've earned it!

Chapter 11

JUST ANOTHER RUBBISH TEACHER

> If we are taught by teachers who lord their intelligence and power over us, when we take up our own teaching posts, do we imagine that we are now all-powerful? Do we feel like frauds if we play at being powerful? Or do we recognise that nobody has education all worked out?

Teachers all over the world retreat into the staffroom and offload about their difficult classes. When I became a leader of learning, many staff would refrain from having these discussions until I had left the room. Supply teaching put me back in the cupboard and I regained my insider view. Unguarded, unprofessional discussions about what the 'little shits' have done today, or how the 'fat ginger kid' is destined for failure, or how much they 'hate' a particular class happen daily.

In places where the students hang out, the same discussions are taking place from the other side of the divide. You will overhear that Mrs A is 'a bitch' or that Mr B is 'the worst teacher and knows nothing'. It is us versus them, unless we can bridge the gap.

Us versus them is not confined to teachers and students. It is also a problem between management and teaching staff. The methods used when leading, supporting or coaching staff are much the same as the methods used with the children. Of course, some staff do

> What's the worst thing you've said about a child or a member of staff? Was there a genuine excuse to say it?

underperform and senior leaders can get frustrated by their lack of results or floundering lessons.

Stop being pathetic!

A leader and a middle manager sat in the corner of the staffroom. The middle manager's face was a picture of concern. 'Luke just flew at her,' he said, describing the scene in his staff member's classroom earlier that day. 'Mrs J was petrified. She called for me right away, but something needs to be done. This was assault.'

> As a manger, have you ever found yourself irritated, angry or absolutely fuming at a member of your staff? What did you do about it?

'What's her problem?' the leader responded in an accusing tone. Concern did not feature on his face. Rather, he was rubbing his temples in a display of stress and annoyance. 'Doesn't she know the behaviour policy? Can't she do anything right?' The leader was not asking these questions of the student but of the staff member who had been assaulted. He was irritated with the middle manager because he had dared to come to him with the problem.

The leader's exasperation, fuelled by his own teacher gremlin, was unhelpful in finding a solution. He was only looking at the situation from his own perspective – that this would cause him extra grief. He was unprepared to take the time to slow down, observe the issue from all sides and look for a solution.

> What wider consequences might occur because of your unhelpful emotional responses to situations as a leader?

Later on that day, the student in question had been given a detention by the middle leader but had failed to turn up for it. The middle leader felt unable to follow this up as he had not received leadership support in the first instance. This left the student free from consequences and free to assault again another day.

What might be the bigger consequences of this outcome on whole-school behaviour? What effect would this have on Mrs J and every other teacher who heard the tale? What impact might this have on the student's understanding of right and wrong? What effect might it have on the behaviour of other students who have witnessed or heard about the incident? How might this shape the relationships between leaders, middle managers and teachers in the school? How might the leader's conduct influence his middle manager's behaviour? Could the leader have avoided this? What should he have done?

Leading others

As a leader or a teacher, asking the right questions, removing your personal feelings, communicating effectively and working together towards solutions always trumps using your power and status to make yourself feel better.

This leader used his power to deflect the situation away from himself. This resulted in negative consequences far beyond the original problem, which would eventually fall right back at his door. It may have made him feel better about himself in the short term as he sidestepped dealing with the issue and put the blame firmly on someone else, but in the long term it caused more problems for more people. The student in question continued his negative behaviour around school. More students began misbehaving once they saw that there were few consequences for poor behaviour. Mrs J eventually left education and the middle leader's negative attitude towards his job was clear for all to see for years to come.

Condition yourself to step into the cupboard in those moments. Don't respond with gut reactions – think! Remove emotion and explore the situation *and* its consequences. Respond with solution-focused questions whenever possible. In what way could what you do today have a lasting effect on the school community or the individual tomorrow? The leader may have been experiencing marital difficulties, sorting out a distressing child protection case or feeling under pressure from their own manager – the list goes on. But there is no excuse for reacting in this way. Becoming a leader is about more than just a pay rise.

Supporting teachers in practice

Coaching teachers is similar to mentoring students. No 'how to' guide is going to teach you how to get it right every time. Coaching requires you to be human first, and that means honing your observation and people skills, taking your own emotions out of the equation and stepping into the cupboard of possibilities with the person you are coaching. Gaining the perspective of the person you are supporting is a must. Removing your teacher gremlin is essential.

A teacher was experiencing such negative behaviour from students that he was at risk of being put on a performance plan and potentially losing his job. The children hated the lessons and the teacher was on the verge of going on long-term sick. This teacher had been teaching for much longer than me (which at this point was around six years). He was a head of department with at least twenty-five years in the profession under his belt. But now, observations from senior leaders had noted behaviour issues in his classes and unsatisfactory teaching. The school management plan was about to go into action and I was called in as a last resort. The leadership team were asking, 'Why can't he just teach properly?' and 'What's wrong with him?' These questions were not helpful – they wouldn't solve anything.

One thing I have noticed in all of my roles is that teachers are no different from students. Whether it is a leader experiencing a problem with a member of staff or a teacher experiencing behaviour issues with a class, asking the wrong questions is unlikely to produce positive results. The calming process that I outlined at the start of Chapter 2 (if emotions are running high) or the

Ladder to Success (Chapter 4) can be equally useful in supporting staff as well as students.

Just as building a relationship with your students can help you to become a better teacher, so coaches need to build a positive relationship with the teachers whom they are supporting. You might read comments in lesson observation feedback, such as, 'Students in the back row are messing about. Be more vigilant' or 'You didn't notice that student B had their hand up all lesson.' Sure, the observer is pointing out problems, but they are not exploring ways to improve practice.

Have you ever been observed by leaders who only know your name because it was next on their list of staff observations? I know I have. The worst observers have an air of self-importance and menace. They sit at the back of the classroom with their clipboard and a disapproving look on their face, ticking boxes. Tick boxes are an attempt to improve outcomes; someone somewhere thought this practice of observation might work. I applaud them for their problem-solving attitude, but I'm grateful that the practice is being phased out. However, we must be aware of what we are replacing it with. When done properly, coaching observations are useful. Leadership observations for the purpose of filling out a spreadsheet are not. Struggling teachers or slipping standards necessitate intervention. It's important to get your choice of intervention right.

Following my analysis of the data presented by the leadership team, my first action with the 'failing' teacher was to take time to observe him in practice. Taking the issues I observed and the questions asked by the leadership team as a starting point, I reframed the information into a solution-focused question: *how can lessons and outcomes be improved while getting the teacher to enjoy the process and grow?*

> Have you ever deemed someone an unsatisfactory teacher based on one lesson?

Observation

Observations always take place in the metaphorical cupboard, which is another way of saying that you need to avoid hearing the opinions of others and instead focus on the actual evidence. Remarks must be sensitive but objective. The main questions I wanted to answer were: 'What is it like to be a student in this classroom?' and 'What is it like to be the teacher in this classroom?' Surprisingly, it was the room itself that struck me most.

Entering with the students, I joined the lesson as they would. There was no clipboard in my hand, just an open mind waiting to be filled. I saw the scruffy displays, the damaged desks and the accumulation of classroom detritus that had built up over the years. This room was unloved and it was screaming disorder. I took my uncomfortable seat and was barked at to behave. I didn't want to. The room didn't inspire me to want to learn. It seemed to symbolise how lost the teacher had become. He had become blind to the mess that was promoting a classroom of chaos. The teacher had experienced so many members of the leadership team sitting in the room and judging him that he saw me as just another young teacher who thinks they know it all, ready to beat him with the 'unsatisfactory' stick.

> Do you ever judge others without walking in their shoes?

Solution

After the lesson, he sat and waited for my assessment. I had already thought it through from his perspective and could see that nothing useful would be gained by allocating a damning grade, so I didn't. I could see he felt ashamed. Shame can be disabling and cause us to want to protect ourselves from further humiliation. His defences were up and he was anticipating discomfort. I wanted to switch this to an anticipation of reward.

I had carefully communicated my plans to the school leaders before the observation, who had agreed that he would have no management observations for a number of weeks to give me time to build his confidence back up. This gave me the opportunity to get to know him properly and prevent the dreaded tick boxes ruining everything I hoped to achieve.

Instead of jumping in with the problems I had observed (and, believe me, there were many), I told him how inspired I was by the potential of the room. I noted its size and the equipment available. Did he have any plans for it? Just like the students in my supply lesson and my problem Year 7 girl, he was caught off guard by something unexpected. I tried to stress that I wanted and valued his opinion. Again, this was not a trick; I genuinely wanted to know what he thought. If you are attempting to get a colleague onside, but are being insincere, they will spot your dishonesty and the relationship will falter.

My feedback was solution focused, practical and genuine. The room did have potential and I was truly excited by the idea of working together to solve the problems he was experiencing. Developing an authentic relationship with someone is not the same as applying a strict method and expecting it to work every time. This becomes obvious from the vantage point in the cupboard.

Testing the solution

During the hour that was allocated to us for feedback, we talked through ideas, ripped everything off the walls, rearranged furniture and made plans for even more improvements. We were collaborating to create a rewarding space for him to enjoy teaching in again. As we were working, we casually talked about lessons we had each enjoyed and what made them so enjoyable. The time was spent doing practical things but it was also spent getting to know each other. If I wanted him to feel rewarded, I needed to know what would be rewarding for him. Each of us has different likes and dislikes; it is what makes us who we are. This process allowed me to get to know more about him, while also breaking down barriers between us.

During breaks, lunchtime and after school, we continued to work together to sort out the space. We improved the ICT in the room and created usable wall displays (similar to the super stuck wall I described in Chapter 10). Thinking from the perspective of students in his lessons, we began to consider what might be rewarding for them. We explored approaches to differentiation and independence by using the space we had created. The wall displays also supported the development of knowledge, and as we were creating them we were able to discuss ways of introducing students to new information. This development was not done to him; he was enjoying the process and much of it was instigated by him. The more excited he got about his space, the more he wanted to show me how he was using it to promote excellent learning.

We continued our regular lesson observations and, because we had developed a working relationship in which feedback was seen as a way to move learning forward, his lessons improved rapidly. At first, we were making big changes but over time the feedback became more about tweaking small elements to improve learning for everyone. His change in attitude towards the students (and his job) – alongside the interesting, engaging and well-pitched lessons – quickly had an effect on student behaviour.

Before long, visitors to the school were being taken via his room to see the excellent learning going on. It was a must-see stop on the tour. The teacher was proud of what he had created, and this pride translated into excellent lessons. Because we had built up a respect for each other as colleagues, he began to be much more open to accepting any teaching and learning tips that would improve his practice.

Review

The original management plan was never implemented and the teacher had his mojo back. Behaviour improved and the students began to love his lessons again. All this from asking the solution-focused question: *how can lessons and outcomes be improved while getting the teacher to enjoy the process and grow?*

By the time the senior leadership team came back with their tick-list, he was proudly in control of his teaching again.

Whether we are working with colleagues or children, we have to see the individual before anything else. Developing a relationship of trust and understanding is the first step to success. You may know exactly what a colleague needs to do to improve, but will simply telling them to do it motivate them to try? Do you understand why they are not doing it in the first place? Do you observe with the intention of labelling that person, or do you observe with an open mind, ready to put the time and effort into making a lasting change to their practice? How does it feel to be your colleague? How does it feel to be their student? What can you bring to the table and how will you present it in a way that seems desirable and achievable to all involved? Whatever you do, make sure you are ready to look from everyone's perspective, not just your own.

Chapter 12

CONTINUOUS PROFESSIONAL DEVELOPMENT

Can you become the best version of you? If something feels pointless, can you find your own purpose in it or do you build yourself a wall of resentment? Can you become your own master when it comes to continuous professional development (CPD) and look at it in another way?

The cupboard view of continuous professional development

My best friend is a joiner-inner. I know that if I have an idea for a day out – no matter how muddy, childish or far away – she's in. She doesn't sit back and watch our kids play, she is hands-on in there. This is why, when I was describing one of my professional development sessions to her, I was shocked by her response. 'You're one of those!' she said, eyes rolling with distain. She meant that I was a trainer who expected audience participation. The teachers who attend my training sessions are always expected to join in. I don't want my students passively listening to me in lessons, so I can't see why a group of teachers should be any different. The response just wasn't like her.

Her dismissive attitude seemed to come down to one simple question: 'What's the point?' As with everything, professional development has to be applicable to your practice. My friend had experienced sessions on topics that she knew inside out, topics that had no relevance to her job and topics that she saw as just plain wrong. She had experienced so much of this kind of training that, like the kids who see no purpose in school, she saw no purpose in professional development. She did not want to join in. How many teachers feel exactly the same way? How many teachers see professional development as something that is done to them, not for or with them?

Having experienced some pretty rubbish professional development myself, I knew where she was coming from. However, the cupboard is not limited to the classroom. Every situation has the potential to become a learning situation, if we can get our perspective right. Just as sitting in the cupboard and observing bad situations can teach us how to put them right, even the worst CPD has the potential for learning, if we ask the right questions. My mantra for professional development sessions in which I can see no immediate purpose is: 'How can this work for me?'

On one occasion, as I sat through the most mind-numbing session, I began to observe the speaker. As he stumbled over his words, sweating profusely, I saw that he was not confident in the material presented – or, if he did know his content, he was not confident in its delivery. I began to explore myself as a trainer using this session as an example. What else could I learn from him? The training was not supposed to be about self-reflection, but by asking, 'How can this work for me?' I turned a potential waste of time into something useful for my professional development.

I noted why I was bored. The presentation was a PowerPoint filled with bullet points that I could not absorb quickly. Furthermore, I was not given a chance to digest what was being said as the only person talking was the trainer. The content was all about another school and what they had done. This would have been more interesting if my colleagues and I could have explored the similarities between that school and our own, but we didn't get the chance.

Of course, he may not have been able to stop sweating for other reasons, but I recognised that an audience assesses your appearance and every move. Take some time to think about how you come across. I know that if I don't have a deep knowledge of a topic, I will probably stumble over my words, so I never turn up unprepared. With a little creativity, we can turn any situation into a learning situation.

The worst ever training session

Teachers can make awful audience members. Imagine a class who talk over you, play on their phones, refuse to take part in activities and roll their eyes because they don't want to be there. You are picturing the average CPD session with teachers! The same teachers would not accept this behaviour from their students, but somehow these rules don't apply to them.

The worst-behaved group that I ever had as a seminar leader was a bunch of behavioural support assistants. Their daily job involved supporting students who had been removed for behavioural difficulties and helping them reintegrate back into lessons. They questioned everything I said (luckily, I know my stuff). Questioning is not a bad philosophy, *if* you are truly listening and applying what you hear to the reality of your situation. It can grow your understanding and practice. However, this group were questioning to trip me up, not questioning to understand. It was a form of attack, not a development of self. Their walls were collectively up and they were playing a game of 'destroy the trainer'. This group was not unlike my nightmare class from earlier in the book. They refused to listen, interrupted me and each other and even made plasticine penises, which they waved in each other's faces!

As the session progressed, I began to get a severe case of fight or flight. One of the quieter members of the group was trying to answer a question, but a group at the back of the room were giggling uncontrollably and playing sword fights with their handcrafted phalluses. I could just quit, walk out and never look back. Instead, I told them all to stop. Mustering my best teacher voice and my

> Have you ever purposefully picked on a trainer?

most composed demeanour, I made the whole room pause. Just as I would with a class who had gone too far, I asked for everyone to be silent and for everything to be put down on the tables.

Taken aback at this young trainer suddenly taking control, they did as I asked. I calmly asked them to look around the room and to think about how the other people around them were feeling. How did the person who was trying to contribute and the quieter members of the group feel in that moment? How were their actions affecting everyone else? They were being self-blind, and I was either going to make them realise that or be ejected from the building (probably through a window).

This could have gone badly wrong. I was determined to get them to see their own walls and the culture of zero learning that those walls were creating. They were acting just like the children for whom they were supposed to be role models – but they did not want to learn themselves. This moment of reflection was powerful, and the rest of the day went off without a hitch. The assistants had opened their eyes to their behaviour and recognised it as the kind they did not want to see from their students. From that moment on, I have never again shied away from having high expectations of the teachers in my training sessions. Likewise, I have always observed my own behaviour in the training room. If I have high expectations of my students, I also have to have high expectations of myself. We are role models and we have to live our expectations.

Any situation has the potential to be a powerful learning experience, but only if you let it. By being self-aware, you can watch your own walls rising and so you can also take them down. If you are told the title of an upcoming training session a month in advance, do you think about how its themes are relevant to your own classroom? Do you consider where you are right now on this issue so that you know what you would like to find out? Teaching is a busy profession, but this isn't hard to do. It takes very little time to think.

For example, you are about to have a session on numeracy across the curriculum. In the week leading up to the session you could note down how you have been using numeracy in your lessons and what impact it appeared to have. You don't even have to write notes — you could do it all in your head, but if you want to be even more proactive with your self-improvement, you can use the Professional Development Diary in the Resource Cupboard. Be prepared for your own learning!

One head of department I used to work for would proudly proclaim that he was 'a reactive teacher, not a proactive teacher'. I was never sure if he understood what he was saying because, as far as I was concerned, this was not something to boast about. If you only ever react and very rarely plan, you may get better accidentally, but you are unlikely to become your best self. It takes very little effort to become aware of where you are with a topic, so you can be prepared to fill any gaps and improve your practice.

When you are in the training session, try to empty your mind, be present and listen. Try to avoid the voice in your head telling you that this is nonsense. Listen to understand before you begin to question. Let the trainer complete their explanation before you put your hand up in the air to argue. Don't switch off. Don't browse Facebook. Listen. Apply what you are hearing to your own classroom and then ask yourself, 'How could that work for me?'

Observation

In any training session, there is always a teacher with a wall of defiance: 'I don't need to know this!' 'This won't work in my subject.' 'I've seen all of this before.' This wall results in a sour face and zero professional development. They have surrounded themselves in cement that can only be cracked if you pour on the right solvent. Telling them won't work — the wall is much too strong for that.

> What walls do you put up when faced with a training session that you don't want to attend?
>
> Do you behave appropriately in professional development sessions?

A business studies teacher who was attending one of my training sessions demonstrated his wall by stating at the beginning of the session: 'There is nothing you can teach me that I don't already know.' I knew that, try as I might, I was not going to even dent his wall. I took a different approach and suggested that if I couldn't teach him anything, then perhaps he could teach me. This was said with sincerity, not sarcasm. I invited him to observe me and to provide feedback to move me forward. I wouldn't say he entered into it with an open mind, but he did leave with a handful of ideas. I had taught him something – and not one single 'I told you so' left my lips! However, I did realise that, regardless of how long in the tooth they are, there is always something new for every teacher to learn. You just have to get the setting right for their wall to melt away.

The wall of defiance is a wall of protection. If, as a trainer, you judge the wall to be impenetrable then you will never get past it. As with anything, if you believe it is impossible, you make it so. Call me an idealist, but I have found success in the direst of situations by having an 'I can' attitude (as well as a rich knowledge base). Ask yourself: what is it that keeps the wall in place? What does this teacher fear? Do they fear change, looking stupid or being less than perfect?

If you are the teacher behind the wall, ask yourself: what is holding it in place? What could I possibly lose from opening up and letting the learning in? Fear is always a building block in any wall. My business studies colleague did not want to be told what to do by someone half his age. He felt more comfortable in the role of observer. From that position of power, his defences came down just enough for him to gather some ideas of his own. Nobody told him to take them; he was in control and no longer needed to stay behind his wall.

What triggers you to put up your wall? Is it training that contradicts what you have been practising? Are you afraid that your practice is now obsolete? Is it a fear that listening will lead to harder work on your part? Is it anxiety about not understanding new developments in education because you

> Do you scoff at CPD that doesn't seem relevant? Do you refuse to learn?

are one of the older members of the group? Whatever it is, find the trigger and do whatever it takes to make this particular wall unnecessary. You don't have to agree with the training, but you shouldn't expect your students to turn up to your class with a thirst for learning if you can't do the same.

The world is changing at an exponential rate: how we digest the media, cook our food, commute, communicate, keep ourselves healthy, solve crimes and, of course, understand the human brain – to name but a tiny fraction of the social and technological advances of the past fifty years – are evolving rapidly. Education tends to lag behind. Does it fall behind because too many teachers have a safety wall around them, and are unwilling to grow and learn? Many conversations overheard in staffrooms would suggest that the answer to this question is yes. Teaching is a tough and time-consuming job. You are just getting to grips with one syllabus when it is ripped out from under you at the whim of a new secretary of state for education. A new initiative, a new syllabus or a new way of working will result in negativity behind closed doors. 'They are making us do this now!' 'They have brought this in – it won't work!'

This cynicism will not necessarily be communicated to the leadership team. The teachers expressing this negativity are often part of the problem. They will fill in the ridiculous spreadsheet that doesn't add up. They will follow the new lesson plan structure when they are being observed – even though they think it makes their lessons worse. They won't bring up problems with the leadership team, and therefore they won't always have the information they need to improve the situation. On the whole, senior leaders initiate change because they want to improve outcomes for all. Teachers need to provide purposeful and timely feedback on those changes to ensure that this is exactly what happens in the long run.

As a teacher, you need to be informed about what you are doing and why you are doing it. You need to ensure that any change is in the best interests of your students and their education. It is not all about you. Change often creates fear, so when a new initiative is introduced in a CPD session, the walls can be up before the speaker has even finished their first sentence. Try to reframe your thinking: there is always something new to be learned. Instead of dismissing the training because 'there's nothing new in this for me', open your mind and ask yourself, 'How could this work for me?'

Try this!

Set yourself a metacognitive wrapper before every training session. A metacognitive wrapper is a way of thinking about your thinking before you start thinking. Simple, right? Actually, it is. There are three questions: the first asks you to review your current position, the second asks you to think about your starting point in terms of action and the final question asks you to reflect on your evidence of learning and what you will actually do with it.

For example, you are about to sit through a teacher training development session on questioning. Here is the wrapper:

1. What do I already know about questioning and what am I already doing?

2. What level of thinking is appropriate to challenge me in this session?

    a. Getting to grips with the basics.

    b. Gathering new ideas.

    c. Applying new ideas to current practice.

    d. Creating new ideas that nobody has ever thought of before.

3. What evidence of learning will I have at the end of this session? (Notes/photographs/short videos, etc.) What will I actually do with it? (Blog/try it out/develop a lesson study group, etc.)

    You may not know exactly what evidence is going to be presented to you but you can be prepared. For example, I always take notes with an old-fashioned notebook and pen, although some people will prefer to use a laptop or tablet. My jottings are not forgotten but are used to plan my next steps and are eventually written up as a blog post. Whatever your preference, make sure you plan to do something with it.

By asking these three questions before any professional learning session, you can always get something out of it. You choose at which level it is appropriate for you to engage, so there is a level of challenge across the range from novice to expert.

Shortly after the session, ask yourself the three questions again, but this time as a tool for action:

1.   What do you now know about questioning that you had not thought about before?

2.   What level of thinking is appropriate for your next steps?

     a.   Getting to grips with the basics – you need to do more reading.

     b.   Gathering new ideas – you need to do more reading.

     c.   Applying new ideas to your current practice – you need to try things out and observe the impact.

     d.   Creating new ideas that nobody has ever thought of before – you just might change the way this is practised!

3.   What evidence of learning do you have, and what will you actually do with it? A notebook filled with ideas going dusty at the bottom of a drawer is no good to anyone. Make a plan to use, share or develop what you have learned so that it has purpose.

Solution

How can we re-engage with professional development even when what is on offer isn't very good? Has your school created a professional development programme that looks great on paper but in reality is utterly pointless? You are not alone. Most school leaders want to do the right thing, but they forget to work with the professional teachers 'beneath' them to make this a reality.

Although having a quirky one-off INSET is beginning to fall out of fashion, I have found that when providing professional development training to schools worldwide, many still want it done that way: come in, perform and then the teachers will take over and apply it in the classroom. To have the most impact on student outcomes, teachers need to work collaboratively and practise what they have learned. The schools and colleges in which my work has had the most impact are those that think way beyond the one-off session. Informed planning sessions take place with key stakeholders before the visit, the presentation day is about staff voice and exploration, staff have time to practise, lesson observations with the 'expert' are built into the year and we frequently review the impact on student outcomes to ensure maximum success.

Do you ever feel like you know a training session is going to be pointless before you have even attended? Perhaps you have been to some related training previously, it is a topic you know inside out or it is on an area that has no relevance in your classroom, but you are forced to attend anyway? If this is the case, your school has got professional development very wrong. They have a one-size-fits-all programme that ticks their boxes; once ticked they can move on.

> Do you give in to a lazy school culture to fit in?

This kind of training is the least effective way of nurturing professional development. As I've mentioned, you can always get something out of a training session, no matter how poor. But even with my mantra, 'How can this work for me?' you have to work very hard to find the gem of wisdom to take away from this type of session. If you are not a leader, it is difficult to do anything about your school-run CPD. However, you can do something about your own professional development. You can lead your own learning.

Testing the solution

Get the video camera out. (You may need permission for this because most schools have a policy on filming children. If your school is forward-thinking and has lesson observation technology already in place, it is likely to be easier to obtain permission than if they don't. Either way, you must get the necessary authorisation.) Set it up in your classroom and leave it there without turning it on for about a week. Initially, the students will be curious about why you have it there. They will ask why you are filming them. Tell them you will be observing learning in some of your lessons so that you can find ways to improve your classroom for everyone. This is an opportunity to have a conversation about being a learner for life. After a week or so, they will lose interest in the camera. Then it is time to begin.

Video a selection of your lessons. Once you have enough footage, sit down and watch yourself in action. The first time I was encouraged to video myself teaching, I didn't have a focus so my responses weren't particularly constructive. When the NQT trainer asked me what I'd got out of viewing myself on camera, I said that I looked fat! You will observe yourself much more objectively if you have a focus, such as the quality of your questioning, behaviour for learning, starter activities that challenge all learners, the effect of a particular tool or resource on learning and so on. In this way, you will know what you are looking for. Your focus should come from the problem that you are attempting to solve, so this self-observation is a way of actively testing your solutions.

It's common to find it difficult to watch yourself at first. You will observe yourself pulling faces you didn't know were even possible, you will zoom in on your crazy hair or strange-sounding voice, but after a while – like the students getting over the

> How often do you evaluate your lessons, looking for ways to improve?

camera in the room – you will get over yourself and be able to concentrate on the learning in the lesson.

Self-evaluation isn't easy but once you get the hang of it and remove your self-blindness, it becomes part of your practice. The video camera is acting as the teacher in the cupboard. You must learn to look through the lens, step back and observe without judgement or defensiveness. Avoid simply watching yourself and giving yourself a label: 'crap teacher', 'stupid voice', 'too animated', 'too vague'. That label can begin to define you; instead, observe to improve. Try to focus not on yourself but on the effect of particular actions on your students. 'That description was too vague. Would it be helpful if I prepared more examples to accompany my descriptions?' This kind of objective critique will move your practice on much more quickly than simply labelling what you do as wrong. You could use the Video Critique pro forma in the Resource Cupboard to help you.

Before

Remember that the intended outcome of your observation is to improve learning in your classroom. Which areas of learning do you expect to see positively in the video? Which areas do you think may need to improve?

Examples: questioning, direct instruction, group work, student learning behaviours, visual examples, use of resources, lesson opener to engage, lesson dosing reflection.

- Positive – Students A, B and C will be on task
- Negatives – The rest of the students will take time to settle and interrupt learning often. This will not allow us to get through everything quickly.

During reflection

Were you correct in your predictions above? Explain:

Predictions were correct. Noticed that the starter task did not settle as hoped. Two students take up all my time with corrections. Whole-class discussions are only contributed to by students A, B and C.

From your own observations, list the improvements you would like to make in order of most to least likely to impact upon learning outcomes:

Starter task, whole-class discussions contribution, avoiding the need to correct two students (this is taking up the most time and so would be the most valuable if I can improve it).

What questions are arising in your mind as you watch?	Attempt to answer …
How can I engage all students at the start?	Rewards could be my focus instead of sanctions. Immediately reward students who do everything right at the start of the lesson.
Am I ignoring rewards in favour of sanctions?	Yes!
What is causing the two students to ignore the rules?	Students are getting attention from me in negativity. Begin to only notice the positive around them and observe the impact.
Am I rewarding students with negative attention?	Yes!
How can I seat the group to stop interruptions?	Focus less on seating and more on rewards for positive behaviour.
Why are the students not engaged? Did they really understand that task?	After marking the work, they did complete the task correctly. Off-task students as well as on-task students. Up the challenge – including support for those who are less confident.
Would a visual example have kept their minds focused?	It's worth a try!

Here are some suggestions for self-reflective questions, but try to make up your own too:

+ How often am I the one talking?

+ Are all the students engaged? Why? Why not?

+ What kind of questions do I ask?

+ How do the students respond to my questions?

+ Am I involving all the students or do some students get left behind?

+ Did my starter have the desired effect?

+ Were the students able to learn what I hoped they would learn?

+ How effective is my lesson opener?

+ How effective is my lesson ending?

The list could go on, but try to zero in on what could lead to improved learning in your lessons and not on details about you or your appearance. You are looking for an avenue to investigate, not a reason to quit teaching. As you begin to answer your questions, consider which area is likely to have the biggest impact on student outcomes if you investigate it further. Remember, you are looking for an interesting question that will help your professional understanding to grow.

For example, you might find that your questions are only receiving one-word answers, and you are accepting them. A good way to begin to address an issue like this is to write down everything you observe about questioning in your classroom. Now you have your starting point, you can investigate and collate a portfolio of ideas and research into questioning in the classroom. This need not take over your life. Choose one of your free periods or an hour after school on a quiet day as your own professional development time. Research articles, blogs and YouTube videos to add to your collection of information. Then you can begin to practise.

> How often do you try out a new strategy, watch it fail and give up altogether?

Don't throw everything at your classes in one go. Take things slowly, one change at a time, so that you can observe the impact of different strategies for your chosen investigation. Your aim should always be to improve the learning in your lessons and increase student progress. Continue to video your lessons, watching them back to observe how the strategy affected the outcomes. This professional development can last for as long or as little as you like. You could focus on one area for one week or investigate an area of your choice in depth for a number of months, if you are enjoying it and continuing to improve as a result. Nobody told you to do this, so nobody is going to tell you when to stop.

Some forward-thinking schools already embrace this kind of professional development. They recognise that teachers can lead their own learning and can grow at their own speed. If the culture of your school is to put up with boring, repetitive and one-size-fits-all training, but you still want to grow as a practitioner, use this method and watch yourself develop. Choosing to have professional development done to you is actively encouraging your wall to grow and your brain to numb. Take control of it and show your leaders what you are capable of.

More solutions

If the culture of your school is negative, it might not take long before it drags you down too. One school I worked in had NQTs acting like they were on the verge of retirement and had seen it all before. They would dawdle on their way to the CPD room and make sure that everyone around them knew exactly how bored they were. I had delivered CPD at this school years before I went there on supply and one teacher had actually fallen asleep, such was the culture among the staff. They believed that the school was dreadful, that the children didn't want to learn and that CPD was something being done to them. It was grim.

> What would constitute your ideal professional development? Have you told your senior leadership team?

During my time as a supply teacher, I feared that the school's culture had the potential to pull me down too, so I decided to take control. Starting small, I made my targets two young teachers who taught in nearby classrooms. My mission was to get them talking about teaching and learning, to get them excited to learn. To begin with I ensured that every conversation I had with them about what the students had been doing in my classroom was positive. These were simple ideas that they could use too. They were grateful for the resources and tried them out for themselves.

Next, I told them that I was supposed to review two teaching and learning books but I didn't have the time, so would they like to do it for me? I had chosen Will Ryan's *Inspirational Teachers, Inspirational Learners* and Isabella Wallace and Leah Kirkman's *Feedback*, which I knew they couldn't help but enjoy.[1] They agreed, read them and tried out some of the ideas. When telling me about what went well, I could see their attitudes were changing. My relentless positivity was beginning to rub off on them. Before long, we would spend lunchtime like a little teaching and learning group, discussing ideas and swapping notes on things we had tried. Our voices carried and soon others began to join in too.

I am not suggesting that this small action revolutionised the school, but I am saying that it was worth it. If those positive conversations were enough to bring joy to even one of the classrooms in that school, that was a great result in my eyes. If your school is a den of negativity, do something about it! Don't get sucked into that toxic culture. First of all, put the brakes on. Look around and see where the positivity can begin. Keep it small at first, but be relentless and watch it grow. Why would you want to work in a depressing environment? Why would you not want to enjoy what you do and help others to enjoy it too? As social beings, our default is to fit in. We don't want to be seen as different because that could lead to us being excluded. However, a negative-culture school will not thrive. Be part of the antidote to pessimism; collaborate and help others to bring about a more welcoming space in which people want to learn and grow.

---

1   See Will Ryan, *Inspirational Teachers, Inspirational Learners: A Book of Hope for Creativity and the Curriculum in the Twenty-First Century* (Carmarthen: Crown House Publishing, 2011) and Isabella Wallace and Leah Kirkman, *Best of the Best: Feedback* (Carmarthen: Crown House Publishing, 2017).

Collaborative CPD can be extremely rewarding. If you have managed to convince just a handful of colleagues to get on board the positivity train, you can begin to work with them on projects that can demonstrate what is possible to the whole staff. Why not collaborate on an investigation into engagement, behaviour, assessment or any other avenue that could improve classroom teaching and outcomes for all? Why not choose something that everyone is complaining about and plan to make it better? Don't hold yourself back. Use the Clarity in Collaboration pro forma in the Resource Cupboard to help you and a colleague get started on making the changes that your school so desperately needs.

During my time as a supply teacher, I have not yet found a school in which teaching and learning is perfect. Teachers moan about the management, managers moan about the teachers, children moan about it all. What I have observed is that most of the dissatisfaction comes from people who see things as they are, not for what they could potentially be. If you want to change how CPD is done in your school, take some control. Show the managers what you are capable of. Demonstrate that you can work professionally to improve your classroom practice and the learning for your students without any need for direction. Don't dally away CPD time on being bored and vacant – step up!

> Do you ever use gained time to collaborate?

If you complete a project successfully or if you establish a collaborative group that is making changes for the better, let people know what you have done. Infect others with the need to be lifelong learners by publicising the impact of your actions. Remember why you are teaching – to change the lives of the students. You are not going to do that unless you keep up to date and make the most of your learning opportunities. Be a great teacher and develop yourself professionally – for life!

Try this!

Next time you are about to sit through a CPD session, try out these actions before, during and after. Try to recognise your walls and overcome them with a view to growing and learning.

Before

How am I feeling about this session? Why do I feel this way?

How am I already using the topic that will be covered in my own teaching?

What do I hope to gain from this session?

Where is my wall when it comes to this session? How will I see it coming?

During

Recognise resentment, switching off, anger and challenge. Ask yourself why you are feeling that way. You are beginning to put up the wall. Can you take it down before it sets firm?

Put all personal feelings out of the picture. Empty your mind, be present and listen to understand.

Make notes on things you did not know or things that feel important to return to. Don't make notes on everything. Try to remain in a listening-to-understand state of mind.

After

Return to your hopes from before the session. Don't feel angry if they have not been fulfilled. How can you deliver on those hopes yourself without resentment?

Return to your notes on your current practice. What will you do differently now as a result of what you have learned? What are your next steps as a learner and practitioner?

Return to your notes from the session and use them to make a plan for classroom action. Don't try to do everything at once. Do one thing at a time and measure the impact of your actions.

Don't give up after a week if things don't improve. Continue to reflect on the thinking you did before the session about your hopes in this area. You can take action to improve with further investigation.

Review

Just as applying what works with one well-behaved class to a horrendous class can be unhelpful, applying 'how to' solutions to the problems we face won't work in the same way twice. Being a teacher isn't easy; you can't pick up a single book that will give you simple solutions to getting it right. If we could, the world would be a much more harmonious place. Even with all the knowledge and expertise in the world, things can and will go wrong. That's what makes the world interesting! If we approach problems with this understanding, we can feel less shame and learn more about ourselves and our practice.

As a new teacher, I thought silence and attentive-looking faces meant I had cracked it. Over time, I realised that creating a culture of learning – in which good learning behaviour is the norm – had much more purpose than getting the buggers to behave.

The difficulties that can spoil our jobs as teachers are myriad. However, the one constant that I have observed is that when teachers stop blaming and start thinking through the eyes of their students and colleagues to find a solution, even the worst of situations can improve. We are all only human, we make mistakes, but we also have the capacity to change, grow and be amazing!

During those bygone times when I sat in the cupboard, I observed a lot but took little action. I always had an excuse ready: 'I'm just 21.' 'I'm just a classroom assistant.' Excuses led to me doing nothing. When I finally stepped out of the cupboard, it was time to take control. Blindly following protocol serves nobody, no matter what stage of your career you are at. If we observe schools continuing to fail the students most in need; if we are merely spoon-feeding those who can take it; if we see leaders treating those 'beneath' them badly; if we are writing off struggling teachers; if we are complaining about issues without doing anything to change them – then *we* are to blame. It's time to stop making excuses and become part of the solution.

Step into your own metaphorical cupboard and ask yourself: when children behave badly, what is the reason? When teachers teach badly, what is the cause? When leaders fail us, what are they missing? When we get it wrong, how can we change? Remove the blinkers, look around and see how you can master the problems in your school and beyond.

Perhaps you started reading this book with a problem in mind, a problem you felt you could not solve. My sincerest hope is that the real-life stories and creative solutions shared here have given you some new ways to move forward. Even the most hopeless situations don't last forever. The power to change things doesn't rest with someone smarter, higher up, more connected or braver. It rests with you! There is always some small action that you can take, as long as you see yourself as being able to take control. Sure, there will be consequences, but that is just the next problem you'll have to solve. You are setting up your own desirable difficulties – and that's the way you are going to continue to learn.

It's time to let go of the belief that it's better not to try so you are guaranteed not to fail. Nobody has the world of teaching all worked out. All we can do is our best to achieve what is good and right. Here's a thought: in 100 years we will all be gone. What will be left as a result of your time on this earth? A lifetime of bitching and wishing, or a lifetime lived with creativity and change? It is up to you!

The examples in this book come from real, lived experiences in which creativity, taking action and self-control led to positive outcomes. We all have the capacity to take action. We can all question to create. We can all take control of our own emotions and how we treat those around us. We can all make a difference. We can all be great teachers!

THE RESOURCE CUPBOARD

The following resources have been used to successfully develop thinking and enhance learning. Use them, play with them and adapt them to suit your learners' needs. The resources are downloadable from:

https://www.crownhouse.co.uk/featured/teacher-cupboard

Have fun!

Question Stem Cards

Get students asking their own questions. Teach them how to formulate questions and allow them to play and create. Don't be scared of your students' questions – questions can change the world!

Is it right to … ?	What if … ?
Does it matter if … ?	Why is it that … ?

When is it that ... ?

When is ... ?

Where did ... ?

What could happen if ... ?

How can ... ?

Are there ... ?

Moving Forward Conference Cards

When all seemed lost, the moving forward conference helped me to find a way to start again with a nightmare class. Use these cards to structure your first lessons with students or to help you begin a much needed conversation with a problem class of your own.

How can we develop a group that:

Shows respect towards each other, **learns loads** and enjoys our time **together**?

The conch

Traditionally used to allow democracy.

The holder is the only person permitted to speak.

If you are not holding the conch, you must listen before you react.

To request the conch, raise your hand and wait for the speaker to pass it to you.

Grice's maxims

Quality: Truthful and respectful.

Quantity: Turn taking.

Relation: Listening and responding – building upon the points of others.

Manner: Politeness, eye contact, back channelling.

Moving Forward Conference

Basic rules – do we need to add to these?

- Respect the rules of the conch and the speaker; listen to what they have to say by emptying your mind.

- Keep hands, feet and objects to yourself; respect others' personal space.

- If what you have to say could hurt someone's feelings, consider keeping it to yourself.

Anyone breaking these rules will be removed from the conference and held for an extra hour after school.

Class Manifesto

The following points have been created together as a group.

This will be typed up to create a class manifesto.

All members must sign and agree to this.

Format of Moving Forward Conference

1. A question is posed.

2. The conch holder is the first to respond – everyone else must respect and listen to the speaker.

3. The conch is then passed to someone with a raised hand (the choice is the conch holder's).

4. The conch is passed until everyone who wants to respond to this question has spoken.

5. A conclusion is drawn by the lead conch holder.

6. The group should all agree with the solution and this will become part of our class manifesto.

1. Very little learning was able to happen last lesson. What caused this and how did you feel?

2. What would have made things better last lesson?

3. What, from your perspective, makes a good lesson?

4. What rules would you like to put in place to make sure that our class is calm and productive?

5. What consequences should there be if anyone breaks our rules?

6. What questions do you have that may make a difference to our group?

SOLO Taxonomy

Learning about SOLO taxonomy helped me to plan my lessons more effectively, develop strategies for differentiation and help learners to understand their own thinking. This article, originally published in *Innovate My School* magazine, can help you to get started with SOLO thinking in your own classroom.[1]

A Beginner's Guide to SOLO Taxonomy

The Structure of Observed Learning Outcome (SOLO) taxonomy aims to show pupils how to develop sophisticated responses to questions by getting them to examine their thought-process as their understanding of a topic improves.

SOLO defines five stages of understanding for any topic: prestructural, unistructural, multistructural, relational and extended abstract. The first three involve gathering relevant information. The other two are about using that information: linking facts and findings, questioning existing ideas about the topic and forming new theories.

All well and good. But how does it work in practice? Here's a simplified example of how SOLO can help a pupil with little knowledge of a topic to develop a sophisticated understanding of it and see the thought-process that got him there. In our imaginary lesson, the goal is for pupils to write an essay exploring the choices Johnny Depp has made in his acting career.

---

1   Originally published in the September 2012 issue of the digital magazine, *Innovate My School*. Available at: http://www.innovatemyschool.com/ideas/ going-solo-an-introduction-to-the-taxonomy-everyone%E2%80%99s-talking-about.

Prestructural

Pupil response: I think Johnny Depp is a Shakespeare character because we watched a film featuring both of them.

To move on: The pupil must begin to gather basic information on the topic. He has clearly not understood that Johnny Depp is an actor, and knows of no choices Mr Depp has made.

Unistructural

Pupil response: Johnny Depp acts in films.

To move on: The pupil has understood one choice Johnny Depp has made, but there is no further detail. The pupil should conduct further research into the actor's career and the different roles he has played.

Multistructural

Pupil response: I know lots about the life and times of Johnny Depp. I know the films that he has acted in. I know that he dislikes mainstream films. He has acted in some mainstream films.

To move on: The pupil must begin to make links between the information he has found about Johnny Depp's life and the choices he has made as an actor.

Relational

Pupil response: Johnny Depp is a popular actor who first came to our screens in the 1980s. At this time, cinema was very popular. Johnny, however, decided to shun the bright lights of Hollywood, opting instead for less mainstream roles, in films such as *What's Eating Gilbert Grape?*

To move on: The information gathered has been linked contextually. The pupil should analyse and question his findings, and draw his own conclusions about what he has discovered.

Extended abstract

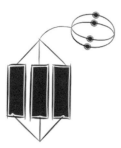

Pupil response: Johnny Depp is a popular actor who first came to our screens in the 1980s. This was a time when cinema was very popular. Johnny, however, decided to shun the bright lights of Hollywood, opting instead for less mainstream roles, in films such as *What's Eating Gilbert Grape?* Was this conscious decision to avoid the limelight actually just a clever tactic to engage the interest of potential fans from niche groups? Let us look through his career history to find out …

To move on: The pupil has linked his knowledge, examined it in greater detail and theorised about Johnny Depp's choices. He should always seek out new ways to develop and apply what he has learned.

Implementing SOLO

By providing a clearly defined path to higher order thinking, SOLO makes self- and peer-assessment easier. In my experience, with various year and ability groups, including sixth form and bottom sets, once pupils have been taught the features of each SOLO level and how it leads to the next, they are quickly able to use the system to develop sophisticated ideas about almost any topic.

Because it is a highly structured approach, SOLO must be introduced accurately. Ensure that you fully understand the idea before using it in the classroom. Create examples like those in this article in order to establish how the approach can be used within your subject. If you are confused, what hope do your pupils have of 'getting it'?

In particular, pupils must recognise the differences between the levels and the importance of each level. Multistructural may be a 'lesser' form of understanding than relational, but it is a necessary precursor to it: one cannot relate multiple facts without first gathering them. Be sure to explain each stage's place in the sequence of thinking. If pupils already have good knowledge of a topic, they may need less time for multistructural research, but it is still necessary to acknowledge its importance – if only for when they encounter a topic about which they at first know very little.

It is also important that your initial question is accessible, and that it enables pupils to develop their answer to the extended abstract level. When I first used

SOLO with my Year 9 class, I began by posing the question, 'Did Shakespeare write every story ever written?' A typical response was 'No, but he wrote lots of plays.'

At this point, I introduced SOLO and explained that such a response was unistructural if correct, but prestructural if it missed the point.

Next, I explained that the pupils' existing knowledge of Shakespeare (not their single-sentence answers but the other things they already knew) was multistructural. I got them to write everything they knew about Shakespeare and his plays on large pieces of paper, and I gave them some further facts before we moved on.

Having thus established multistructural knowledge, we moved on to relating the facts and ideas they had written down. I asked the pupils to compare Shakespeare with a modern writer and to use their knowledge of Shakespeare's times and modern times to compare and contrast the work of the two writers.

Finally, I asked the pupils to question their findings further. I provided them with question stems to encourage them to explore various points of view about the comparisons they had made. By questioning their relational ideas, they were able to start creating new, educated conclusions about their explorations.

This extended abstract stage can be reached only when the pupil becomes knowledgeable enough about a topic to hypothesise about it with logic and evidence. Pupils are unlikely to reach this level in a single lesson.

The benefits

One-sentence or single-word answers are common responses from pupils, and we usually accept them if they are correct. After grasping the principles of SOLO, however, pupils begin to think more carefully about the quality of their answers. They realise that one-word responses are unistructural and therefore less valuable than answers that draw links between several facts or observations.

To get the most out of SOLO, use it widely and daily. It can be applied to many tasks, such as setting desired learning outcomes and assessing the level of thinking that has gone into pupils' work. You can also give pupils instant feedback on their oral responses by using the symbol for the SOLO level that an answer has reached. The more I use the approach, the more valuable I find it.

Worst/Best Ladder to Success

Use this resource to compare reality with what you hope to achieve (see page 64). Explore learners' current behaviours and create a ladder towards behaviours that you want to see. Don't expect them to magically change. Help them to climb the ladder!

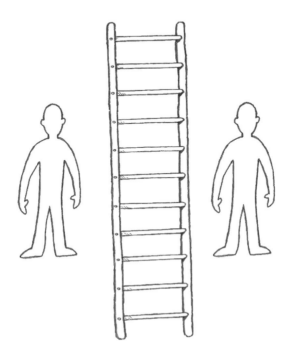

Thought Bombs for Divergent Questioning

This group of statements were the original thought bombs used in a lesson that supported students to think for themselves, question assumptions and become more articulate. Notice how the statements are unexpected and explode the original train of thinking. What would your divergent questions be? How could you create similar statements that shatter your students' current way of thinking?

Robert is retired.

Robert was born in Stockton and grew up in Middlesbrough.

Robert's father's family came from India in the 1700s. Several of Robert's ancestors were brought over to Britain to replace dead seamen on the trip back from India and became stranded in England.

Robert's mother's family were poor and worked as servants in a large stately home in Yorkshire.

Robert hates his children and uses fishing to get away from his family.

Robert attempted suicide last year.

Robert left his job under a cloud of suspicion.

Roberta works for a blood diamond charity and has raised thousands of pounds.

Roberta worked as a doctor but gave up her work when she got married. She decided that she wanted a family and began to foster children a year after marrying her husband, Bruce.

Roberta's family have lived in Nottingham for three generations. Her parents still live in the house she grew up in.

Roberta fosters disabled children.

Roberta has one child of her own.

Roberta survived breast cancer last year.

Marni is originally from Sunderland but her father, an electrical engineer, relocated to China when she was 12. She has lived there ever since.

Marni had an affair with her citizenship teacher.

Marni is pregnant.

Marni's child will grow up to be an evil dictator.

Marni is a convicted killer.

Marni sabotaged the ship.

Robert had fish and chips for tea.

Roberta had a salad for tea.

Marni had meatballs for tea.

Conjunctive Adverb Cards

Use these cards alongside blank hexagons to support your students in becoming more articulate. They can be used to help them develop arguments, structure speeches and write essays.

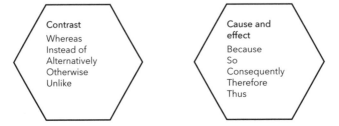

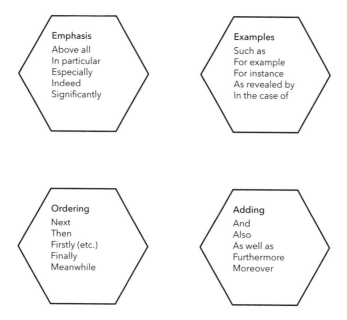

Procrastination Hotspots

Rank yourself from 1 to 5 (1 – strongly agree, 2 – slightly agree, 3 – neither agree nor disagree, 4 – slightly disagree, 5 – disagree).

Type		1	2	3	4	5
P	You take at least half an hour to write an email.					
P	You agonise over a single word in a document for ages.					

Type		1	2	3	4	5
P	You waste time trying out fonts, background colours, etc. on a PowerPoint for a single lesson.					
I	You are due to deliver a presentation to the school leaders. You can't stop thinking about how they will judge you. You put off doing anything.					
I	The thought of showing a senior member of staff your work fills you with dread. You avoid the task to prevent them seeing your faults.					
I	You wish someone better than you had been asked to do a particular task. You delay working on it to hide from the guilt.					
M	You would rather tidy your whole house than start this task.					
M	Every time you think about the task at hand you get bored. You avoid it!					
M	The sun is out … you succumb to the temptation to shelve the task entirely.					
O	Thinking about the task makes you anxious. You avoid it!					
O	You can't see how you will get the task done in the time you have. You avoid it!					

Type		1	2	3	4	5
O	Huge tasks make you stressed, so you get all of the little jobs done and avoid the bigger tasks.					
L	You always leave tasks until the last minute.					
L	You work better when your back is against the wall.					
L	You always get it done in the end, so you choose having fun over getting it done early.					

P: Perfectionist

I: Impostor syndrome

M: Motivation (lack thereof)

O: Overwhelmed

L: Lucky!

Time Diary

Time Diary		
Date	Aim	
Time	Activity	Notes

PLTS Log

Creative **Thinker**	Independent **Enquirer**	Reflective **Learner**
Team **Player**	Effective **Participant**	Self-**Manager**

You are learning to learn

- Be reflective.
- Join in.
- Work with others.
- Be creative.
- Behave well.
- Learn from mistakes.

Be the best you can be!

My skills record

Date:

Name:

Dreams:

Professional Development Diary

Don't wait to be told to improve your teaching and learning. Take control and master professional development for yourself. You can use this planner to help record your progress and focus your thinking.

Date	Observation/question/ focus	Actions	Resources/further reading

Video Critique

It can be difficult to know what to focus on when videoing your lessons. Use this guide as a starting point to target your thinking.

Before

Remember that the intended outcome of your observation is to improve learning in your classroom. Which areas of learning do you expect to see positively in the video? Which areas do you think you may need to improve?

Examples: questioning, direct instruction, group work, student learning behaviours, visual examples, use of resources, lesson opener to engage, lesson closing reflection.

During reflection

Were you correct in your predictions above? Explain:

From your observations, list the improvements you would like to make in order of most to least likely to impact on learning outcomes:

What questions are arising in your mind as you watch?	Attempt to answer …

Clarity in Collaboration

Use this pro forma to support your collective focus on joint projects.

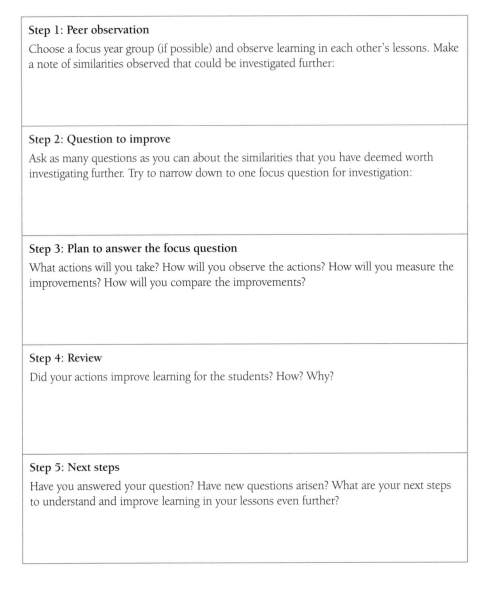

Step 1: Peer observation

Choose a focus year group (if possible) and observe learning in each other's lessons. Make a note of similarities observed that could be investigated further:

Step 2: Question to improve

Ask as many questions as you can about the similarities that you have deemed worth investigating further. Try to narrow down to one focus question for investigation:

Step 3: Plan to answer the focus question

What actions will you take? How will you observe the actions? How will you measure the improvements? How will you compare the improvements?

Step 4: Review

Did your actions improve learning for the students? How? Why?

Step 5: Next steps

Have you answered your question? Have new questions arisen? What are your next steps to understand and improve learning in your lessons even further?

Self-Observation Tool

This tool can help you to focus on what is actually happening in your lesson. Stop allowing emotional reactions to cloud your thinking and focus your energies on making improvements to your practice.

	Notes	Learning barriers caused	Questions arising
Entering the class			
Individual tasks			
Group work			
Peer interaction			
Adult interaction			
Information from other adults			
Home understanding			
Actions based on observations:			

BIBLIOGRAPHY

Allison, Shaun and Tharby, Andy (2015). *Making Every Lesson Count* (Carmarthen: Crown House Publishing).

Ashes, Lisa Jane (2012). A Beginner's Guide to Giving Students SOLO Autonomy, *Innovate My School* (September). Available at: http://www.innovatemyschool.com/ideas/going-solo-an-introduction-to-the-taxonomy-everyone%E2%80%99s-talking-about.

Ashes, Lisa Jane (2014). *Manglish: Bringing Maths and English Together Across the Curriculum* (Carmarthen: Independent Thinking Press).

Berger, Ron (2003). *An Ethic of Excellence: Building a Culture of Craftsmanship with Students* (Portsmouth, NH: Heinemann).

Biggs, John B. and Collis, Kevin F. (1982). *Evaluating the Quality of Learning: The SOLO Taxonomy* (New York: Academic Press).

Bjork, Robert A. (1994). Institutional Impediments to Effective Training. In Daniel Druckman and Robert A. Bjork (eds), *Learning, Remembering, Believing: Enhancing Human Performance* (Washington, DC: National Academies Press), pp. 295–306.

Brown, Peter C., Roediger, Henry L. and McDaniel, Mark A. (2014). *Make It Stick: The Science of Successful Learning* (Cambridge, MA: Harvard University Press).

Crosson-Tower, Cynthia (2013). *Understanding Child Abuse and Neglect*, 9th edn (Upper Saddle River, NJ: Pearson).

Dweck, Carol S. (2006). *Mindset: The New Psychology of Success* (New York: Random House).

Frederking, Robert E. (1996). Grice's Maxims: 'Do the Right Thing'. Presented at the Computational Implicature Workshop at the AAAI-96 Spring Symposium Series, Stanford University, 25–27 March. Available at: http://www.cs.cmu.edu/afs/cs.cmu.edu/Web/People/ref/grice-final.pdf.

Hook, Pam and Mills, Julie (2011). *SOLO Taxonomy: A Guide For Schools. Book 1: A Common Language of Learning* (Invercargill, New Zealand: Essential Resources Educational Publishers).

Jaffe, Eric (2013). Why Wait? The Science Behind Procrastination, *Association for Psychological Science* (29 March). Available at: https://www.psychologicalscience.org/observer/why-wait-the-science-behind-procrastination.

McFall, Matthew (2018). *The Little Book of Awe and Wonder: A Cabinet of Curiosities* (Carmarthen: Independent Thinking Press).

Milgram, Stanley (1974). *Obedience to Authority: An Experimental View* (New York: Harper & Row).

Navarro, Joe and Karlins, Marvin (2008). *What Every Body is Saying: An Ex-FBI Agent's Guide to Speed-Reading People* (New York: HarperCollins).

Nuthall, Graham (2007). *The Hidden Lives of Learners* (Wellington: New Zealand Council for Educational Research Press).

Peña-Ayala, Alejandro (ed.) (2015). *Metacognition: Fundaments, Applications and Trends* (Cham: Springer International Publishing).

Ryan, Will (2011). *Inspirational Teachers, Inspirational Learners: A Book of Hope for Creativity and the Curriculum in the Twenty-First Century* (Carmarthen: Crown House Publishing).

Tice, Dianne M. and Baumeister, Roy F. (1997). Longitudinal Study of Procrastination, Performance, Stress, and Health: The Costs and Benefits of Dawdling, *Psychological Science* 8(6): 454–458.

Wallace, Isabella and Kirkman, Leah (2017). *Best of the Best: Feedback* (Carmarthen: Crown House Publishing).

West, Edie (1997). *201 Icebreakers: Group Mixers, Warm Ups, Energisers and Playful Activities* (New York: McGraw-Hill).

Willingham, Daniel T. (2009). *Why Don't Students Like School? A Cognitive Scientist Answers Questions About How the Mind Works and What It Means for the Classroom* (San Francisco, CA: Jossey-Bass).

Zimbardo, Philip (2007). *The Lucifer Effect: How Good People Turn Evil* (New York: Random House).